Color, Facture, Art and Design

Artistic Technique and the
Precisions of Human Perception

T0167905

Color, Facture, Art and Design

Artistic Technique and the Precisions of Human Perception

Iona Singh

Winchester, UK
Washington, USA

First published by Zero Books, 2012
Zero Books is an imprint of John Hunt Publishing Ltd., Laurel House, Station Approach,
Alresford, Hants, SO24 9JH, UK
office1@jhpbooks.net
www.johnhuntpublishing.com
www.zero-books.net

For distributor details and how to order please visit the 'Ordering' section on our website.

Text copyright: Iona Singh 2012

ISBN: 978 1 78099 629 5

A CIP catalogue record for this book is available from the British Library.

Design: Stuart Davies

Printed and bound by CPI Group (UK) Ltd, Croydon, CR0 4YY

We operate a distinctive and ethical publishing philosophy in all
areas of our business, from our global network of authors to
production and worldwide distribution.

CONTENTS

Acknowledgments

I would like to acknowledge those who have supported and contributed to this book over the years sometimes without even knowing it.

Valerie Bayes, Jack Ameriglio, Joel Kovel, Karen Charman, Agnes Tedman, Marion Hasson, Najma Abbas, Jeffery Steele, Gary Tedman, Peter Townsend, Ken Voyce, Susan McCrae, Joseph and Noella Tripetti, John Evans, Diane and Steve McHenry, Claire Weldin, Francoise Caselles, Pierre Cadiou, David Ruccio, Eric and Eleanor Clark, The Teachers Benevolent Fund, Jo Kirby and Ashok Roy - National Gallery Conservation Department, Ann Hulland, John and Annie Singh, Arthur Wilson, Bridgette McCarthy, Croydon Youth Theatre Organization, Clore Gallery Library, Joyce Townsend - Tate Gallery Conservation Department, The Rijksmuseum - Holland, Georges and Noelle Perceau, Suzanne Sbidan, Colin Parkinson, Estate of Mary Martin, Paul Martin, Charmalene Asha Catania, La Famille Brousse, Michael Parsons, Maurice Dennis.

Preface

Art is guarded. Art is in cities. Art is often in old established buildings. It can seem very bourgeois. The bulk of art gallery visitors are from the middle-class. All characteristics that lend suspicion as to what side art takes in the class struggle. How do you approach it if you are a socialist but still love it? Why do you like it? Are you secretly a turn-coat? Are you not really a socialist but hanker unconsciously for an elite world beyond yourself? Are art works really something, or are they just another product of hype and overpricing in the universe of consumerism and stock exchange values? How many times have I stared at the Vermeer in the National Gallery London and asked, do I think this painting is good just because I know it is worth fifteen million pounds and because it is surrounded by guards in black uniforms? I asked, am I really seeing something on that gallery wall or am I just dazzled by an illusion that this little rectangular canvas is quite rare and beautiful?

After asking this question for a number of years I came up with an answer: "*Yes*". Yes I think these paintings are worth something, are beautiful and rare. Having studied fine-art and having pretensions to making some good works of art myself I came to realize that the materials that go into a painting have some very strange effects. This is not really mystical; just the product of different colors and pigments on the senses. This book is an attempt to find this aspect of paintings, not to dissect the beauty and magic of them by their practical origin, but to understand this in a material sense. Theorizing in this way does not dissolve the mystique of art, but explains it in terms of materials and its material affect on the body. The magic extends from the subtleties of nature to the precisions of human perception.

I always thought the atmosphere in art galleries to be very

nice. This sense starts from the works of art and seems to move outwards through the room and walls to all the facilities, café, toilets etc. even to the dress sense and presentation of artists and those working closely with it. This is the affect of having a cared-for object or objects in the vicinity. Intensified sensual entities made just for the human body and its outreach faculties. What a contrast to the big exterior world, the majority of the present-day designed and built environment where color, texture and shape and their effect on the human eye, body and feeling are sacrificed to commerce and lumpen brash economy. This abuts the world of art as if the two environments are diametrically opposed. Sometimes a kind of class policing on both sides even excludes one from the other and this policing extends to attempts to analyze the situation, to theory. Here we try to avoid this by bringing art out of its placebo environment to demonstrate its links to science, physical perception and the limitations made on it by the tools of the trade: the art and design materials produced under the current conditions of production. It is easy to write about art in poetic terms but this is often too abstract and limited by its own beautiful self-referentiality and produces practical and theoretical obstacles for a material holistic method. This needs to be avoided because real clarification of the subtle alienating effects of much of popular culture itself is distinguished by the most 'non-applied' discipline of the art world: fine-art, and its writing companions in art history and theory. The latter rarely encourages art as a sensual and dialectical process, i.e., from nature and for us in nature. This effect has several repercussions. It deprives socialism of a thorough materialist critical conception of art by creating a void in art theory for present day communist parties throughout the world and for socialist and communist societies in the future. This void is the unspecified area of the relationship of ideology to art from a sensual, physical and materialist viewpoint. This void obfuscates the details of the process of the reproduction of the means of production on the

2

level of feelings, via the aesthetic level (Tedman 1999). It leads to a series of relatively feeble and politically neutral critiques that overlook the profoundly subliminal affect of media such as television, advertising, pop music and cinema. Marx and Engels never denied the affect of superstructure on the base and alluded to the fact that reactionary art, media and oppressive environments are all part of the same process that stem from the same economic oppression.

A prime difficulty and failure to transgress this alienation in art and art theory, and to incorporate both a physical and rational aspect persists even now, perhaps because art operates at the level of feelings. Everyone is submerged in their own romantic tendencies, desires and choices regarding art and any challenge to them can be very destabilizing. So it is difficult, impossible even, to write from outside of popular culture, by looking into it and judging it except perhaps for the possibility of a keynote: fine-art, as a sort of gateway to a different type of aesthetic universe. Albeit a largely conjectural keynote put into place as a phantom sensed out from small chinks of light breaking through from the art of the past, different societies and small progressive caveats found in contemporary art and design departments and practices. With these foundations however one can construct a whole world and step into it. The construction of an argument, a philosophical stance, poem, musical composition, book, novel, or painting can be so far away in time and space but so close affectively, empathized and lived. The language and grammar of artists in the form of materials and technique are used succinctly to accommodate these affects and this is well studied in literature but vastly looked in the realms of art. The focus here is on the form of the work and its potency beyond time, space and ideology because of its appeal to the relatively slow-changing formal vehicles of perception, entities that must be taken into account along-side ideology. To ignore this is idealist, a denial of Einstein's theory of relativity; of the observation point of the body in space that changes the perception of time by its very presence.

This is an attempt to break art down into its essential components, a bit like Jean Piaget's *Structuralism* project. If one traces the route between each discipline correctly, from the machinations of the "purest" component of the art world, fine art, this can then be applied to other related and "applied" disciplines, studies in popular culture, architecture and design. The importance of this in societal change is still underestimated forty years after Althusser's initial concept of the reproduction of the means of production. The necessity of breaking it down and theorizing the galaxy of art and design is as necessary as it is political because the question of socialism and aesthetics is so far only partly answered.

Introduction

As an art student I knew works of art had to be constructed, usually in a studio with paint tubes, pigments, resins, canvases and stretchers and disheveled artists and students struggling to make something meaningful with the shapes, colors, substances and ideas. This contrasted wildly with visits to art galleries where there was no sign of this labor. The lofty spotlessness, ornate frames and hushed reverence, all scrutinized by guards, negated the origins of the toil involved in the arrangement of the materials in the paintings. I knew these two forces stood in contrast and that between them they harbored many forms of political and social struggle. The frosty gallery atmosphere served to negate egalitarian access of everyone to the benefits of art and from the acknowledgment of their specific contribution to its production in the social formation. These are class divisions and class antagonisms evident by the confinement of art galleries to major cities, by faux refinement and the unspeakable physical labor that make the artworks everything they are. This book sets out to analyze this space, a vacuum, of how the real, dirty, messy, obscene material artistic labor of love contrasts with the theoretical, non-practical and ideological description and presentation of it. These are the missing details of the extraction of art materials from the natural world to be reprocessed by artists to serve the senses. Most useful in this task are materialist philosophers and their sophisticated descriptions of our relationship with nature; Abelard, Spinoza, Schaupenhauer and particularly Marx, who carefully ground all his ideas within these relationships. Marx and Engels were comprehensive in their attempt to describe our place in the cosmos and relationship to nature and each other. Part of the demonstration of this relationship between humans and nature entails a description of the methods by which we take what we need from it in order to live. The way we obtain everything, food, housing and fuel, without which there can be no philosophy or art. Marx uses the term 'the economic base' to explain the methods by which we transform the raw materials of nature to satisfy these necessities. A key aspect of this process is the work involved in accomplishing it, the labor. Any positive action in life, practical activity, thinking, invention, relaxation, fantasizing and dreaming can be construed in its end purpose as labor either as the direct physical transformation of the materials of nature or by the advance of our comprehension of it and conjecture into its possibilities, to make it more malleable for our purposes. The terms material base and the mode of production are the fundamental economic and social transactions that demonstrate the relationships between labor and nature.

Particularly within the realms of thought, many disciplines exist that contribute to understanding natural processes and how eventually to manipulate them. A vast selection of these studies unite in Marx and Engels's method of analysis, their philosophy: dialectical materialism.[1] It takes us to the fundamentals of these processes and how best to observe them. The basis of dialectical materialism is that the body, senses and intellect of humans, everything, was formed by nature. Thus the evolutionary formation of humans is entwined with all the other animals, natural phenomena, substances and transactions on the planet. This was a slow process, little by little, over millions of years, the species grew, altered and mutated to what it is today. The body, the senses, like those of every other substance and animal that lives, or ever lived, grew out of this. It is an interaction, a to-ing and fro-ing, a chemical progress wrapped up in sunshine, rain, foliage, fauna, minerals and insects. Senses, physique, thinking and language all originate here. So in our formation and mechanisms we are a sort of organic mirror image of nature, an edging forward of its movement, a flowering at its edges.

There is evidence that the senses particularly are permeated with these transactions. Not only the apparent senses, the visual and auditory, tactile and olfactory, but a sensual melangé inside the body forming the fundamental facilities for nuance and unconscious feelings. The pertinence of peripheral vision is one example of how many signs and signals function unconsciously. Signals from it often completely by-pass conscious vision and go directly to parts of the body that do not ostensibly deal with vision. Information is passed through unconscious corporeal routes to inform all levels of consciousness of ideas and feelings that seem to uncannily originate from nowhere. They are a formative link between the finer echelons of the external and internal mechanisms of the body, the visual, oral, tactile and the cognitive facilities of the psyche. As Freud explains, the body is a sunken hyper sensitive tissue covered with a protective skin over its surface as a shield against the harshness of the environment, leaving only a few sensitive samples on the surface in the form of the five senses. Inside we are a sensual cauldron, no senses are separate but connect together and the stimuli gathered from one route can change pathways and inform other internal facilities such as one of the other senses or thought, consciousness or the unconscious. Our bodies are an organized dynamic with the mind and ideas yielding the more abstract sensory conclusions in the form of the rational. So the world of unconscious feeling gives rise, at least partly, to information and sense knowledge that appears to come from thin air because it is unconscious or pre-conscious. This has sometimes been observed or acknowledged in the past as immaterial, supernatural, telepathic, witchcraft or occult until it was eventually grounded by Freud in the somatic.

Artists use these subtleties of perception in their work. Like witch doctors they manipulate the materials of nature and organize them to stimulate the senses. They seize the very substances that enhanced and motivated the body in evolution and combine them in particular formations to construct works of art. Starting with the surface on which to paint; cave walls gave rise to wooden panels and eventually wooden frames and then canvas. The excellent artists of antiquity preoccupied themselves with the whole art object including all the substances underneath the paint. These are the all-important under-layers of grounds which were found to have an intrinsic effect on the work as the all sensitive unconscious eye and sense detects its nuances. Artists soon began choosing their colors and textures very carefully. The substances that were ground up and bound as under-layers made all sorts of changes to the paint on the surface. They seemed or could be interpreted to have an almost mystical affect; the substances are there but can hardly be seen directly as they begin to stimulate the transactions of perception to inform the whole body, not necessary consciously but as feeling and abstract ideas that seem unconnected. Small wonder that art still has a transcendent magical quality imposed on it that, even today, after Einstein, Freud, Marx and Darwin, remains a dominant feature of art theory.

Paintings that stimulate the senses, body, mind, the unconscious and the conscious use substances from nature in order to prepare for us intensified blue-prints of our sensual relationship to nature. The very best artists have always been aware of the primal, subterranean aspect of this and have always sought to comprehend it at a material level. Using the real materials of nature that are inextricably intertwined with our evolution to awaken these faculties to full potential. The practice of art here reverts again to the quest to understand a relationship to nature as the desire to manipulate and ultimately to make it work in harmony with us.

The name for this exploration, based in the visual sense, is the discipline of fine-art. It is the uncovering of the stimulation of our body and senses in relation to substances and stimuli from the external world. The origins of this discipline as we said, are found in the materials of nature. As with all production, the raw materials and their transformation into works of art, are part of the general transactions of expropriation from nature involving labor and are therefore part of the material base. The study of the production of art, fine art, therefore always needs to include a study of the material base and the rules and formulas of these transactions. Exactly in the same way as all of philosophy and scientific investigation is ultimately founded to uncover the relationship to nature in its profound and harmonious aspect. The more sophisticated this information is, the better we are at extracting the benefits and of actually knowing what they are.

Dialectical materialism, as we said, takes its starting point from nature and from the expropriation of it by labor and of how thoughts and ideas relate to this. The pertinence of philosophy to economics for example is demonstrated in works such as *The German Ideology* to show that economics, the conditions of labor, have a profound influence on philosophy and also that philosophy has great influence on economics. So we find that the economic base and superstructure that comprise ideology and the humanities disciplines including art are indisputably related. The relationship, the precise details of its influences and effects have been open to dispute almost since Marx and Engels first wrote about them. How do the components of base and super-structure relate to each other to keep the whole system turning? Louis Althusser shed light on the reproduction of the base and superstructure as it continues on through time and as we go about our daily management and existence. To explain this he emphasized the role of ideology and what he called *ideological state apparatuses* to describe the affects of ideology on the subject and so define its role in "the reproduction of the means of production." For artists and those working in disciplines that deal with the senses, the emphasis on ideology here as the product of ideas is a little too conscious, linguistic-based and does not quite adequately describe the realm of the senses and their contribution. Gary Tedman (*Aesthetics & Alienation* 2012) has attempted to ameliorate this by taking clues from Marx's own work, particularly the enigmatic *1844 Economic and Philosophical Manuscripts*. On account of the emphasis on the eccentric formal arrangement of this particular work Marx is here considered as a poet and an artist as well as a writer. In this case Marx defined the meaning of his work through writing and language but also *crucially* by the form. This is the form that ties in and emphasizes the language, it is the sculptural setting that gives the work its complete meaning. The study concludes that Marx's *Manuscripts* were written in a particular "eccentric" topological manner that in short serve to emphasize his words through the material construction and arrangement of the pages. Marx the writer therefore expressed certain modernist principals by his technique.

Tedman has explained this formal "three dimensional" expressive device used by Marx, incorporating the use of materials as well as language, as a means of creating a sensual affect in the reader. Thus drawing attention to an aesthetic meaning for Marxism, based in sense and feeling, which is hitherto largely unexplored. Tedman claims that the design of the *Manuscripts* has a slight formal influence on the way they are read and divulges the methodology to enable the location of the role of feelings and sensuality in Marxist theory. Thus defining sense and perception as part of an aesthetic level in the relationship between the base and superstructure and in the *"reproduction of the means of production"*.

Freud himself was also on this track. In *The Uncanny* he writes:

"It is only rarely that a psycho-analyst feels impelled to inves-tigate the subject of aesthetics, even when aesthetics is under-stood to mean not merely the theory of beauty but the theory of the qualities of feeling. He works in other strata of mental life and has little to do with the subdued emotional impulses which, inhibited in their aims and dependent on a host of concurrent factors, usually furnish the material for the study of aesthetics." ... "Good as nothing is to be found upon this subject in comprehensive treaties on aesthetics, which in general prefer to concern themselves with what is beautiful, attractive and sublime - that is, with feelings of a positive nature - and with the circumstances and the objects that call them forth, rather than with the opposite feelings of repulsion and distress."

This is an emphasis on aesthetics as feeling and senses and their heightening or likewise their oppression and dulling - as anesthetics. It enables a radical exploration of sense-based disciplines and is particularly apt for analyzing art because of its emphasis on feelings as part of the corporeal body as formed by nature. Tedman similarly interprets Marx's concept of alienation as the physical and psychological estrangement of the sensual body from nature and thus from its own self as itself a part of nature. This succeeds in removing many transcendent, humanist and spiritual connotations associated with the term 'aesthetic.'

I contest that alienation itself functions in the discipline of art history to generate a failure to incorporate a sensual physical aspect to the theory of art. As the last bastion of immateriality, it is likely to be so, given the subtleties of perception and unconscious thought and feeling involved. Art can easily be mistaken and heralded as godly, transcendent, a semblance of the old alchemy remaining in the twenty-first century. Some of this difficulty persists certainly because art operates at the level of feelings and this is a serious problem for workers in the industry. The general realms of art and culture involve vulnerable personal emotion, affections, memories and sense reactions; elements that are painful and even disorientating to challenge and antagonize. These are the values of a lifetime instilled through the dominant economic base, tradition and personal history, and at this level any challenge to these feelings becomes political. Contemporary culture is difficult to really critique and understand because everyone is writing from the "inside", even theorists need to tune in and turn off to the escapism of popular culture; pop music, cinema and celebrity culture, as a release from daily pressure as a cultural "soother".

An example of how relationships between people, the material base and art materials effect art objects can be found in the work and production of the artist Vermeer. The choices Vermeer made for his work are no longer available to most artists. Like others of his era he spent the first seven years of his career making and acquiring materials for his trade; digging and scrapping them from the earth and the sides of mountains; burning and processing them to make pigment. Today students in college are encouraged to take a tube of paint off the shelf and start painting. Off-the-shelf paint has extra oil added to prolong the shelf life and thereby dilutes the power of the color. The type of oil added to tube paint is usually linseed and under these constraints one is faced with far more difficulty to come up with an original surface and therefore a unique feel to the work, such as Vermeer himself achieved. He would also have been fully conversant with pigment grinding techniques using pestle and mortar or glass slabs to extract color. In this process artists and students of Vermeer's time were able to make a precise choice of paint binder, noting how it interacts with other materials to determine the overall affect of the work. In total a great deal of information of many colors, oils and resins would have been at Vermeer's disposal to account in part for the quality of his production.

One factor that unites most major artists is that they are all interested in the tools of their trade and are keen to experiment to find the right combination for their particular purpose. This means mistakes and mishaps but the experimental nature of their work is also often not very well documented. The first chapter *Vermeer, Materialism and the Transcendental In Art*, is an attempt to give insight into how this particular artist approached his materials at a time when there was more of an intimate connection and before industry intervened in that relationship. We will explore why Vermeer's work is often defined by its transcendence and spirituality but *not* by its material construction. Linking the processes of construction and technique to the aesthetic appeal of the work is necessary because materials and their deft manipulation by the artist form the very appeal of the work. Techniques are elements that bridge the concepts of the artist with his own physical interaction and with the works themselves. If executed well art materials merge with ideas and the sensual interaction of the artist to finally affect the viewer thus providing an interface between the reactive substances of the body and the exterior natural world. A provocation at the most basic and profound level and on which rests the figurative, symbolic, narrative, ideological endowment and eventually the politics and policing of the work of art.

How can the sensual information regarding materials construed from fine art be used outside of the "art" world and the controlled environments of galleries and museums? Is it destined to remain the requisite of an exclusive few or could it help to improve the world we live and work in? Chapter 2 *Color, Facture, Art and Design,* ponders the very profound nature of perception, its manipulation by artists and their materials and renders the application of this to the world of the designed and built environment. Focusing on the example of industrially produced color we scrutinize visual perception that has evolved to discern thousands or millions of shades and colors and is fully integrated with the countless textures and substances of nature. Minerals, plants, moving objects, sky, lakes, rivers and seas are each elements with their own unique colors and textures. The artist chooses material extractions from these and reorganizes them to intensely stimulate the subtlety of perception as it has developed through these phenomena over millennia. We find all this is in contrast to the modern designed and built environment in which many people, those in cities, spend twenty-four hours a day. This environment is limited to a few dozen colors and a few dozen textures such as are made available by the contemporary limitations of the production process. We argue that this severely limits visual and sensual perception in the extremity of its potential elicitation, from nature and from some works of art. This limitation is therefore part of a sensual alienation or estrangement of the subject in the realms of design. The possibility also emerges of transgressing the limitations of production merely by vaguely altering the mode and means of production. The example given here is the work of the French artist Yves Klein. He utilized the modern industrial technology of color manufacture without the modern pressures of the mainstream capitalist mode of production, speed and cost effectiveness. The work that Klein produced under these conditions demonstrates the possibilities of using industrial technology to produce art works whose pertinence has expanded in the fifty years since their creation and will perhaps eventually endure to be on a par with the masters of antiquity.

The previous chapters refer to the ability to perceive color as it effects the whole body in a homogeneous and systematic manner. *Visual Syntax* explores this in more detail as the physical affect of art materials or design materials on the sensual body. Theoretical examples are derived from diverse disciplines to illuminate the function of the perceptive senses and their profound integration. Concepts are drafted from linguistics and mathematics to uncover the nature of the effect of color and ultimately of art. It delves beyond vision and ideas to the holistic domain of the complete physical body to include the rational and the physical. We use the example of a painting by Paolo Uccello, *The Battle of San Romano,* to demonstrate a consciously organized systematic aspect to color relations and how these are advanced with the sensual use of materials to make the painting successful.

This process again includes technical skill and aspects of the manufacture of colored pigment, oils, gesso and other materials and their complementation as they are applied to the canvas. It demonstrates that artists such as Uccello, work sensitively in the application of the systematic nature of color so as not to impose vulgar formal structures onto color perception. The result is a holistic physical unity and the expression of the sensual potential of the body particularly summoned through this.

The study of the contribution of women to art entails a discussion of gender from within the mode of production and the relationship of this to culture. Drawing on the ideas of Jacqueline Rose and Judith Butler, *Women, Culture, Class, Labor* explores the relations of gender to the relations of production. Beginning with the use-value of 'typically' female labor and its relationship first to the dominant mode of production and the conciliation of this with alienation in the mainstream labor process, it concludes that these relations entail many contradictions that boost the meaning of gender. These origins are reinforced by the fashion and the cosmetics industries and further through mass popular culture. Ultimately this serves to redirect sublimated creative energy already alienated by the mode of production. The result is the denial of the relationship between the female and the physical world including her own body and libidinal creativity. It concludes that gender is derived from a fundamentally genderless use-value that is worked up by the alienated mode of production. However, the plastic potential of sexuality that is constantly molded and changed partly in relation to economic and social situations, functions as a subversion against its prohibitions and becomes plausible when based on Freud's concept of bisexuality.

Aesthetic World In The Future conjectures the production of art to a time when different relations of production exist. It examines how these new relations will effect and affect the production of art and the designed environment. The basic premise here is that art is the mediator between the mode of production and the sensual subject. This space in our current system of capitalism is vacuous and difficult to negotiate therefore the production of art in its full sense is equally tortuous. But with this distance lessened through changes in the mode of production, the whole production of high art would itself become far simpler. It would ripple out from the fine arts to architecture, design, objects in the environment, interior design and fashion. These disciplines would become relatively akin to works of art, and works of art themselves would lose their exclusive, 'heavenly' and rare properties. The mass culture of such a system would be closer to what we today call fine art and the rarity that is now high art would relatively diminish. The possibilities of art brought into the environment on a highly disseminated scale is demonstrated by an examination of the mid-twentieth century architect Jean Prouvé. Prouvé had limited success intervening in the mode of production to create industrially produced prefabricated housing that maintains high aesthetic and design qualities even throughout the industrial production process.

The final chapter; *J.M.W. Turner as Producer,* charts the work of Turner as that of an artist who used materials to stimulate human perception in his particular era. We observe his struggle within the contemporary mode and means of production as an artist working in early industrialized Britain in the late eighteenth and early ninteenth century. This was the period when new industrialized methods forced the separation of artists from their materials both physically, by the mechanization of the production process, and in terms of skill; through lack of training and education. The removal of the control of art materials from the art and craft guilds and into the grasp of the large industrialized manufacturers resulted in the ceasing of the artist to have 100 per cent control over the medium. We chart Turner's attempts and eventual successes in surmounting these difficulties, resulting in works that through their concept and employment of materials affect the whole body of the viewer in a physical relationship that includes the mind. As with the work of Vermeer the duality of Cartesian divisions become virtually redundant as Turner's works begin to counteract the estrangement of the labor process, in general society and from within the artistic domain.

I

Vermeer, Materialism and the Transcendental in Art

2001 was the occasion of the *Vermeer and the Delft School* exhibition at the National Gallery, London, one of the most popular shows ever held at the gallery. It was difficult, however, not to notice that the publicity and promotional materials surrounding the exhibition were saturated with references to the spiritual nature of the paintings, and specifically with regard to the work of the most famous Delft artist, Jan Vermeer. To Marxist and materialist theorists of art, this kind of presentation, although widely accepted, is sometimes disagreeable and also perhaps frustrating.

As many materialists will know, the dominant history of art is suffused with references to the spiritual aesthetic. For instance, Rene Huyghe, a member of the Academie française, argued:

"Soon one comes intuitively to understand that every painting is a sign and that one can discover in it the *imprint of a soul*, as one discovers it in a face, as well as beauty and a familiar likeness. Among all the elements that go to make up a picture, whatever they may be, it is the soul that establishes a secret link between them all and makes them one. Painting is not just the approximate image of the world, it gives us the impression of another world, the universe of the painter." (quoted in Hadjinicolaou 1978, emphasis mine)

The following passage from Gombrich (1984) is a specific reference to a painting by Jan Vermeer. It, too, is referred to in this way, as spiritual, uplifting, beyond the mundane, even beyond the corporeal:

"It is hard to argue the reasons that make such a simple and unassuming picture one of the greatest masterpieces of all time...But few who have been lucky enough to see the original will disagree with me that it is something of a miracle. One of its miraculous features can perhaps be described, though hardly explained."

Further on he says:

"It is in the way [Vermeer] achieves complete painstaking precision in the rendering of texture, colors and forms without the picture ever looking labored or harsh...[He] mellowed the outlines and yet retained the effect of solidity and firmness."

This describes the picture formally but still leaves the question of the "miracle" outstanding; there is a jump from precision, textures, and colors to the miraculous. The first part of this second quotation could equally well refer to a photograph, and the latter part to a soft-focus photograph.

Elsewhere, in the *Oxford Dictionary of Art* (1988), for example, Vermeer's work is referred to as having great harmony:

"Vermeer painted those serene and harmonious images of domestic life that for their beauty of composition, handling, and treatment of light raise him into a different class of Dutch genre painter."

This author then describes the paintings as like "crushed pearls melted together," and says that later Vermeer's lost some of their "magic". There is then a brief mention of the broad strokes and variation of textures, with which that statement goes some way toward explaining how Vermeer differs from his contemporaries, but the question of the pearly glow and magic is not explained.

Also in a recent National Gallery press release on Vermeer:

> "The unprecedented degree of illusion he achieved in his
> serene interiors makes his works some of the most *mesmerizing*
> images of Western European art."

Terms like 'mesmerizing' seem to be quite acceptable to use with
painters such as Vermeer, and there is apparently no need to
qualify them. It has the tone of the common language, the
common belief. I think these comments are in earnest, however,
as I too believe that Vermeer's work and the work of some other
artists sometimes evoke an experience that is extraordinary and
that they generate an effect not found very often in every-day life.
The key to this, I believe, lies in the one thing that is invariably
omitted or marginalized from all of above comments, that is the
way the work is *physically constructed*. Vermeer's manipulation of
materials in painting is historically treated as a subsidiary factor
when, in fact, it is central to understanding the work. The
harmony of the forms are well documented, but not so how they
link with the construction. The work needs to be looked at as a
historically made material object, in all its corporeality, and not
just as a picture plane and an illusory image.

Marxist Approaches to Art

When Marx and Engels defined historical materialism, they gave
history a grounding which in the end is determined by the
economic base. However, the precise way that the economic base
relates to the (ideological, political, cultural) superstructure has
been deeply contested among later Marxists. My position is more
favorable to Lenin (against economism), Benjamin and
Althusser's non-humanist approaches, but is extended specifically through the recent work of Tedman (1999). Tedman's work
develops Althusser's concept of the reproduction of the human
subject specifically through a relatively autonomous aesthetic

level. This level accommodates the role of feelings in the repro-duction process. This entails a rejection of Althusser's natural language-centered epistemology which, in turn, was based on Lacan's reading of Freud, in favor of the formation of the subject through the bodily and sensual. Like Tedman (1996), I think Walter Benjamin's thesis in his essay *The Author as Producer* provides the foundation for a more in-depth discussion of Althusser's notion of the traffic or mediation between the base and superstructure. This is based on Benjamin's critique that mentality and ideology alone are not enough to analyze the role of the work of art and its political tendency within the base/superstructure relation, and that a sense element is also necessary to do this. This discussion specifically focuses on the means of production and the forces of production of the base and how these become manifest in the superstructural cultural product, the work of art, via the technique and the sensual mediation of the human subject. As a method this is used to trace the position of the artist, in this case Vermeer, within the framework of these relations (the means of production and the forces of production), and to examine his use of materials and the technique as a sensual practice within them.

I would like to offer this analysis in the light of technical evidence I have gathered regarding Vermeer's painting methods and materials. From this I hope it will become clear that the occlusion of the sensual element and the role or technique in art history is instrumental in enabling a transcendent theory of art to persist, not only in mainstream art theory, as mentioned above, but even within many Marxists or materialist critiques, such as the work of Bourdieu, Jameson, Hadjinicolaou, and Clark. My argument is that the comprehension of the role of technique helps to deconstruct more thoroughly spirituality and transcen-dence (in art history). This is the transcendence that Benjamin refers to as the ritualistic nature of art and Althusser as the strain of humanism within the old ideological universe.

The notion of sensual practice, the aesthetic level, has already been detailed more fully in Tedman, including the defense of this level against the humanism usually associated with the term aesthetic. Therefore I will not be recovering all of this here. Also, although we use and discuss some of the narrative and pictorial elements of Vermeer's work, the main focus is on materials and techniques. Therefore, some well-known elements of narrative and pictorial construction and of symbolism have been left out as they have already been discussed more thoroughly by authors elsewhere.

This Method

In order to accomplish these aims I will first describe the general mode of production of Vermeer's time, focusing on the guild structure in which his practice was formed. I will then examine the technical construction of one of his paintings and the effect that this produces in the finished work and, consequently, in the viewer. The findings will be emphasized by examining Vermeer in relation to his contemporaries and relevant historical figures.

We start by looking at the economic mode of production.

The guild system of production still prevailed in seventeenth century Holland when Vermeer lived, but Dutch merchants who had mapped out trading routes all over the world were a new and growing class of capitalist. As Marx says in Volume 1 of *Capital*, Holland was a model capitalist nation in the seventeenth century, and it was also scientifically and technologically advanced, particularly in textile dyeing processes and in optics, where it was a world leader. In the Dutch guild system all artisans and craftsmen of the time had to be members of the local guild in order to practice, and Vermeer worked within the structure of the artists' guild of St. Luke, in Delft. Every member had to serve apprenticeships of about six years before they could join, and part of this would have been an exploration of pigments, paint making, and related technical skills. Within the guild system every craftsman was seen as on a par with every other, and painters were considered more or less on the same level socially as all the other trades. Vermeer would have met and exchanged knowledge and ideas with ceramists, glass makers, weavers, dye specialists, binders and printers.

However, the Dutch guild structure was beginning to be threatened by the competing influences of the rich merchant class who, while importing raw materials from the Dutch colonies, also began to attempt to participate in the manufacture of goods. While, as Marx says, the guilds thwarted any attempt by merchants to intrude on the guild rules of restricted trade or to break down the separation of the workshops, the merchants nevertheless evaded these rules by setting up their own workshops away from guild control at sea ports and various points in the country side. This allowed the transgression of guild rules, the deregulation of trade and the guild apprenticeship system.

In conjunction with this, the guilds throughout Europe were also under pressure from technical innovations. These innovations were leading to the gradual mechanization of the artisan skills practiced by the guilds, such as weaving and bookbinding, as they were "reduced" to division and repetition. This meant that the fine arts which could not be mechanized were beginning to be separated off from the other craft guilds. Fine artists began to be regarded as more elite and of higher status than artisan craftsmen. In Vermeer's time this process was already widespread in Italy and took the form of artists' academies which were set up in opposition to artists' guilds and were often directly instrumental in their demise. The situation affected Holland when the town of Dordrecht, Leiden, The Hague, and Utrecht all formed artists' associations dissociated from the guilds. The craftsmen's guilds in Delft would have been aware of this process. Utrecht in particular had a large bourgeois art-buying population and was only thirty miles from Delft. The merchants of Delft itself were also becoming important purchasers of art within the town. In resistance to this however, it is notable that the artists' guild in Delft remained true to traditional guild principles, and painters continued to embrace the artisan environment and influences. On its fiftieth birthday in 1661, the painters' guild in Delft actually reaffirmed their commitment to their original 1611 charter of artisan traditions and values. This is despite the fact that the formation of the academies in the towns of Italy and Holland was the first step toward the separation of (what was later to become known as) the "high" or "refined" skill of fine art from artisan and manual skills. This separation is notable as a process that was to continue, and later became more pronounced in all craft and manufacturing as the general process of the division of labor increased.

Materials and Techniques

Not many direct records exist of Vermeer's methods regarding material preparation but the raw materials lapis lazuli, ochres, white lead, and ivory black would have been brought back to Holland by the Dutch merchants whom, by now, had mapped trading routes all around the world. In the novel *Girl with a Pearl Earring*, Tracy Chevalier alludes to the methods that Vermeer probably would have used. As she says, he would have ground black pigment from a piece of ivory and also ground his own white lead pigment by crushing it until it was a fine paste, then burnt yellow ochres by the fire to make them turn red and dark brown; he would have washed, purified, and ground the precious and expensive lapis lazuli to make ultramarine pigment. All this needed a direct and thorough knowledge of what supplies were available, the best new techniques for processing and purifying substances and making them into paint, news of the arrival of new consignments of pigments and resins from abroad and even information about brand new materials that might be of use. Vermeer would have had strong links with other trades specifically dealing with color such as weavers, dyers, ceramists, pharmacists, and printers. Artists were often members of other guilds as well as their own, such as the pharmacy guild.

How would this knowledge have affected Vermeer's painterly technique? I have made a study of the art materials and techniques of a number of historically recognized artists over several years and can give an account of the ground and paint used by Vermeer. The ground is the layers that all painters need to put down on the canvas before the paint. It serves as a background for the paint and prevents it from sinking into the canvas and possibly causing it to rot. It is well known to artists that grounds make themselves "felt" no matter how thick the overlaid paint, as recognized by Max Doerner (1950), one of the few art experts to talk of the physical construction of paintings and of their effect.

The significance of grounds in general and in Vermeer's paintings becomes clearer when compared with different artists. The ground used in the famous work *Giovanni Arnolfini and his Wife*, for example, by another prominent Dutch painter, Jan Van Eyck (1395-1441), was made with glue size, water, and powdered chalk. This produces one of the whitest grounds, and once applied to the canvas by Van Eyck it was polished to become a very flat, smooth surface. Van Eyck began his career as a painter of stained glass windows and it has been said that with the whiteness of his ground, used in conjunction with the oil/resin mix of his paint, he was attempting to recreate the effect of light passing through the stained glass windows of a church. Instead of the religious imagery of the church, however, Van Eyck used the materials and technique to reproduce highly detailed renderings of the lustrous property of the Arnolfinis. Another Flemish painter whose work can be compared to Vermeer is Rubens (1577-1640). His singular ground contained crushed charcoal which makes it bright silver in color. This produces a shimmering effect visible through the paint, contributing to the illusion of movement and "living" flesh in Rubens' work. The characteristics and objectives of Van Eyck's and Rubens' grounds come through into their paintings with each demonstrating the sharply contrasting properties that distinct under-layers can produce. I think their grounds principally serve the pictorial narrative within their paintings and, as we shall now see, in this they contrast with Vermeer.

I made up Vermeer's ground following the ingredients given by the National Gallery's technical department and using approximately the same amounts of each substance as in the original.

In the painting *Lady Standing at the Virginals*, Vermeer's distinct ground is primarily lead white with some ochre, a trace of red lead, a blackish-brown pigment, glue size, and water (Kirby 1997). When these ingredients are put together they make a very unusual and surprising substance. It was quite a shock to find this was under Vermeer's finely painted, luminous, image. Ochres are heavy, earthy pigments made from clay, which maintain some of their rich body throughout the ground making process. Put together with the soft, heavy pigment, lead white, and the other ingredients, they create a grayish-brown combination with a texture that can only be described as like molten volcanic rock. Just as the under-layer affected the works of Van Eyck and Rubens, the gravity and weighted solidity of this ground mixture affects Vermeer's painting and accounts in some way for its gravity and dynamism, despite the fact that the work is just over eighteen inches in length.

But why is the ground gray? According to the psychophysiologist Hering (1964), who based his color theory on the psychological and physiological perception of color, color works in binary oppositions; yellow-blue, green-red and black-white (unlike the Young-Helmholtz theory). Each pair of colors is distinct but works in relation, and one is needed for the other to function. Within this the color gray works as an identity element between all the color opposites. The grayness of Vermeer's ground shines through the colors, not obviously but in terms of a nuance. This underlying tone in the painting is the unifying element that aids the sense of harmony of the colors.

The ingredients of Vermeer's paint are also very distinct. He used Venice Turpentine made from resin from the larch tree, and linseed oil. Add enough resin to the paint mixture and one ends up with an enamel-like, glassy quality. Linseed oil added to Venice turpentine is thick and viscose and can take a large amount of pigment. Intensity of pigment makes intensity of color. The enamel viscosity of the paint prevents the colors from sinking into the dry, dark ground and losing their intensity. The colors sit on the canvas as a homogenous body, with the ground coming through from below. The effect is comprehensive. Take the yellow paint of the woman's skin in *Lady Standing at the Virginals,* for instance. It has a very subtle, bluish-tinge, and it is hard to say whether the color is blue or yellow. Yet the two are psychologically opposite and, in Hering's experiments, cannot be one and also the other. Vermeer's skillful combination of materials stimulates the vision and senses of the viewer and enables a discriminating response.

A great deal is said about Vermeer's representation of light, with critics often confusing his pictorial representation of light with real light, as if real light had entered the painting through the windows depicted in the images. How he achieves this is usually left open, once more adding to spiritual notions about the work, as if he had a direct talent from God that allowed him to recreate light, just as God created light on the First Day. However, on reproducing his materials it is clear that the glassy, resinous paint used in conjunction with the ground has a great bearing on the diffused nature of his canvas hence the description of "crushed pearls". It intensifies in a painterly, tactile, and sensual way Vermeer's concern with perception, visual phenomena, peripheral vision, filtered light and reflection. The paintings are sensual diagrams of these elements so, although the formal system in the painting is that of pictorial representation through perspective, Vermeer is using it to articulate things other than perspective: namely, visual and sensory syntax.

Vermeer's Social-Historical Context

Although Vermeer fitted well into the category of the artistic movement in Delft as one of the new movement of genre painters, vital differences single him out from his contemporaries.

Genre painting arose after the defeat of the Catholics by the Protestants in the long war in Holland against Spanish dominance. All those associated with genre painting, including De Hooch, Steen, Dou and Vermeer were influenced by the new class of art-buying Protestant merchants. The demand was for non-religious or even profane imagery, and for smaller size works suitable for the walls of dwelling houses and not for huge churches. All the paintings of the genre movement take stances regarding the Protestant bourgeois values of hard work and virtue and these are pronounced in all the subject matter, including Vermeer's. However, in some specific ways Vermeer is different and, I suggest, this is the key to his longevity.

The material construction of Vermeer's paintings has references other than and away from the pictorial virtues of the dominating ideology and they work at this level, in contradiction to it. Even the narrative aspect of the images in Vermeer's paintings contributes to this. This is, perhaps, best shown by comparison. There is an interesting inactivity in a painting like Vermeer's *The Milkmaid*, compared to De Hooch's *The Courtyard of a House in Delft*. In the De Hooch there are a number of half-fulfilled events and movements referred to: the woman and child speaking, the broom laid on the ground, in a moment of rest from work perhaps? The door in the wall has flown open: does it need to be shut? The woman standing in the corridor to the left: is she waiting, or dreaming, or talking to someone who is situated outside the house? These questions appear to be De Hooch's main emphasis. The surface of De Hooch's painting is relatively uniform in texture, which allows for these narrative aspects together with the finely detailed depiction of numerous small objects to be focused upon. The painting leads the viewer into the narrative and to conjecture about the possible outcome. The woman in Vermeer's *The Milkmaid* is not, relatively speaking, so much a part of the world of narrative. She is caught up in a moment of time, her face is expressionless, as if dreaming, feeling her way neutrally. The work is not progressing to as many story lines as the De Hooch. The arrangement of forms in the Vermeer, compared with the De Hooch, are more geometric, with larger, flatter areas of color. There are not so many frames within frames in the Vermeer and there is not the same concern with perspective, in which De Hooch's foreground contrasts with the corridor and the open window and door, leading to the view through to the street outside the front of the house. The simpler formal areas and relative lack of narrative in *The Milkmaid*, the combination of the materials, of the ground and paint, are all

constructed to serve and not distract from the visual syntax and its sensual mediation.

These qualities hold true in many other of Vermeer's works where the narrative has been minimized. Geometric shapes along with flat areas of color also prevail in these works. In his painting *Girl with a Red Hat* the out of focus details of the cloak, hat, and chair back are almost totally flat, abstract areas of paint more reminiscent of nineteenth-century impressionism. In *A Woman Holding A Balance, Woman With a Water Jug* and *Lady Standing at the Virginals,* the faces of the central characters are also neutral and relatively devoid of sentimental story-line.

To sum up: I think Vermeer's paintings, through the intricate combination of materials, manipulate the visual senses and perceptive ability of the viewer as a refined and holistic process. It is difficult to understand these effects using the traditional Cartesian humanist terminology of mind and body duality because, I believe, the work operates in opposition to this. I suggest this is accomplished through the physical medium, but not as a "sensory hit", for instance, as Burgin (1986) refers to color without reference to its formal construction and tactile elements. Vermeer's paintings are constructions made specifically for the purpose of manipulating the underlying syntactic elements of color perception in a material-sensual way so that these elements are articulated at their most sensitive and perceptive. I suggest this heightens the senses, including the ability to think, as itself an integral part of the entire physical body. The relative lack of moral or narrative in the paintings does little to intrude on this process by telling the viewer what to think or what moral to follow. It operates almost as if the person viewing the Vermeer painting is a musical instrument and the painting is playing the person, while the person also plays the painting, in a reciprocal musical performance. The body, including the mind, as an interconnecting system is thus being worked upon and is, I think, Vermeer's main concern. Using the abilities of the body in a refined and intense way is what makes our "pleasure" in the works. They create an undermining of the purported separation of thought and the physical, which is a necessary part of the division of labor and is held "natural" by bourgeois ideology. This is in order to legitimate its fundamental division between mental and manual labor. Vermeer's work creates an unusual artistic effect (or general effect) precisely because it is antagonistic to these divisions and does not pander to the dominant mode of production. As with Vermeer, such work is often produced by the artist overcoming great opposition.

This brings us back to Benjamin and Althusser. As Benjamin stated, the work of art may function in counter-revolutionary ways so long as the writer, or visual artist in this case, experiences solidarity with the worker only in the mind and not as a producer, in his sensual labor. I think Vermeer expresses this solidarity through the forces of production, as a producer and in the technique and use of materials which are manifest as sensory elements in his work. Vermeer's position in the relations of production, and the result of this in his works of art, is not part of a mentality or set of ideas but is expressed in the sensual feelings of practice. Hence, Althusser's concept of the traffic between base and superstructure can be mapped out through this cultural production, as it shows an artist's relationship within the means and forces of production, as this transforms by technique into works of art. Using Tedman's (1999) non-humanist account of sensual mediation, the profound physical effect of the work, what in bourgeois criticism becomes manifest as the non-materialist transcendent, can be accounted for and understood in materialist terms as the forces of production and technique as mediated through the human subject, that is, the artist. This materialist understanding can therefore then be distinguished from the enforcement of a non-materialist transcendent which as we have seen functions as part of the ideological and aesthetic apparatus. The aura and uniqueness in the work of art (Benjamin says) as a ritualistic and religious entity retained by the bourgeoisie, overlooks the work of art as a product focusing on the subtleties of perception, knowledge of which Vermeer obtained through progress in optical science together with his training and experience in materials.

Vermeer had a relatively difficult time as a painter with only

33

moderate success in his life. Among the most famous Dutch artists of the day were Cornelius Poelenburgh, a landscape painter who is relatively obscure today, and Godfried Schalken, a realist flower painter. Why is it that Vermeer is accepted as a "great painter" now but was not exalted in his time? I think it is because the ideological position of his work in relation to our contemporary mode of production is no longer as recognizable as it would have been when it was painted. Vermeer's work was relatively overlooked in its time precisely because of his emphasis on construction and the above mentioned purposes it served as compared, for example, with De Hooch's emphasis on construction in order to serve the narrative. Vermeer's emphasis would have appeared very pronounced next to the numerous painters who were appealing more directly to the bourgeois ideology and aesthetics of the moneyed merchant class, such as Poelenburgh and (to a lesser extent) De Hooch.[2]

Today, now that the impact of the contemporary ideological position of Vermeer's work is diminished, it can be recognized and admired for other properties, more slow-changing than ideology. But, as we shall now see, there is still an attempt to assimilate the work into modern bourgeois ideology and aesthetics.

The Contemporary Context

In contemporary art theory there continues a policing of Vermeer that I suggest works on behalf of the dominant class. The policing of the object starts, as we have seen, with a spiritual distortion of the effect of the work in the attempt to forge its materialist elements into narrative, ritualistic aura. This is present in the framework of curatorial and critical practices in which the work of art is embedded, in the effete tones of the art historical descriptions of it, which are then used to support a whole ideological structure surrounding it, from the way art galleries are designed, to the general representation of art in society, and from the spoken word to written articles.

As I stated in the introduction, *the material effect/affect of Vermeer's work is harnessed and presented as something transcendent.* This policing, which includes manners and ways of speaking, encourages caricatures about the uselessness of art, categorizing people alternatively as either effete or ignorant, hence creating common feelings of arbitrary hierarchy and some resentment against art. This policing is, I think, a reaction to Vermeer's painting as a product of artisan construction and skill. To sanction one of the best examples of "high" civilization as the product of manual expertise and construction and not a lofty spiritual occurrence undermines the class that needs to promote the spirit over labor. Therefore, Vermeer is critically still offered today in blockbuster exhibitions like *Vermeer and the Delft School* with the factor of physical construction minimized. The same policing also omits the concept of physical construction of the sensual element of the work of art from many academic disciplines dealing with art. By examining aspects of some principal contemporary Marxist and materialist thinkers, it will be noted in what follows that this policing even interferes here in the form of the occlusion of the role of sensual practice. At this level, these theorists have still not entirely eradicated notions of the transcendent or spiritual.

For example, the Marxist art historian Hadjinicolaou (1978) recognizes that we must "take into consideration the fact that several aesthetic ideologies coexist during any one period and that one of these dominates the others." He also denies "the existence of an aesthetic affect which can be dissociated from the visual ideology of a work," and also that "the reaction varies from pleasure and displeasure and in the case of pictures changes according to the relationship between the spectator's aesthetic ideology and the visual ideology of the work." However, the link between ideology and "pleasure" is not explained, leaving a gap that there is no attempt to fill. He seeks to understand how ideological conditions relate to the position of the art historian and the writer in art, but is it possible that he himself is affected by his place in the division of labor, where the present mode of production also operates in art history?

All art theorists are themselves in the very division of labor of the mode of production that, in this case, Vermeer's work opposes. As a result, theorists are particularly good at deconstructing the narrative of art, thoroughly and with hairline precision, but have made few attempts to deconstruct the painting as a physical object. Writers work within writing and tend to want to write the "story" of the work in its ideological or political context. The visual and aesthetic ideology that Hadjinicolaou does in fact refer to operates at a more profound, sensual, and materialist level than he and other art theorists take into account.

For another example, the (Marxist) art historian T.J. Clark (1974) says that what we attend to in Vermeer is the subtle lack of synchronization between two different interiors, which the dominant ideology wants us to believe are constant, between "the gaudy interiors" of the rooms in his paintings and the "the inner life of the gaze of the main subject". I personally find it hard to agree with this. Are Vermeer's interiors really gaudy? However, *if* it is true, then it is Vermeer's use of materials that brings these contrasts in ideology home to the viewer, that makes them *feel* it physically and act on it physically and not merely as a narrative "going on in their heads" so to speak.

A further example: the work of Bourdieu (1987) sheds light on the nature of the policing of the art object through his analysis of culture as manifest in the struggle between groups with conflicting views determined according to class and education. However, as a solution to the problem of the transcendent or, as he calls it, the "pure gaze" Bourdieu establishes that the work of art has meaning and interest only for those who possess cultural competence and the code that allows them to understand it. This suggests that the code is something taught and "read" as Bourdieu says, according to class, which suggests that Vermeer's works are objects of high art that can therefore be "read" most easily by the bourgeois class. With respect to works such as Vermeer's, this description is, I think, conflating the manners and practices that the bourgeois class possess and that surround the work of art as part of its policing, *with* the work of art on the level of sensual construction and can be construed as the theoretical desire, entrenched in the division of labor, to have it understood that the work needs to be "read" rather than felt.

For my final example, when Jameson (1985) refers to the "end of style" in the work of art, he does so on the basis that style is formed by the unique personality of the artist and their relationship to God. This is a sweeping categorization given for all art yet, at the heart of his comments there persists the non-materialist view of style which has its roots in the spiritual, of style as seen as part of a unique personality and not a skilled and manual job of work developed to have a material affectivity. The proposed solution to this problem by Jameson and others, that is, the attempt to subvert the transcendent element in art therefore omits the role of the sensual element of construction *and* the history of its omission in art theory.

The gap regarding construction and technique in art history can also be construed as part of the "closed reality" spoken of by Derrida (1985). This involves considering an area away from reason, in the sense of the cogito and the transcendent, and toward a set of interconnecting influences in the world. In the production of art this area is often labeled mad (the eccentric artist) and includes *all* the painter's involvement in the preparation of the work, not just the rational and including that of the unconscious. This is because art materials come from an interaction that varies depending on the interweaving of all the forces acting on them as they are made, including the conscious and unconscious, and is also exacerbated by slight difference in the qualities of each particular consignment of raw materials. For this reason, exactly the same ground mixture appears a little different each time it is made. There are usually elements of spontaneity and free play with regard to physical construction which an artist like Vermeer would be aware of and seek to incorporate. The history of art, with its emphasis on narratives, tends to deny this.

Writers and artists often find themselves engulfed in contradictions between the narrative and the sensual elements within the work of art. In the nineteenth century, Proust was instrumental in bringing Vermeer to international critical attention. I think Proust's solidarity with Vermeer arises because Proust, in a literary manner, parallels some of Vermeer's achievements in painting. I include the following passage from *Remembrance of Things Past* to try to convey Proust's awareness of these contradictions and also to give something of an example, in literary form, of what Vermeer achieves in the visual domain. In the book the character of the writer Bergotte, who has spent his life writing popular literature, dies in front of Vermeer's *View of Delft*:

"The circumstances of his death were as follows. A fairly mild attack of uremia had led to his being ordered to rest. But an art critic having written somewhere that in Vermeer's *View of Delft* (lent by the Gallery at the Hague to an exhibition of Dutch paintings) a picture that he adored and imagined that he knew by heart, a little patch of yellow wall (which he could not remember) was so well painted that it was, if one looked at it by itself, like some priceless specimen of Chinese art, of a beauty that was sufficient in itself, Bergotte ate a few potatoes, left the house, and went to the exhibition... At last he came to the Vermeer which he remembered as more striking, more different from anything else he knew, but in which, thanks to the critic's article, he noticed for the first time some small figures in blue, that the sand was pink, and, finally, the precious substance of the tiny patch of yellow wall. His dizziness increased; he fixed his gaze, like a child upon a yellow butterfly that it wants to catch, on the precious little patch of yellow wall. "That's how I ought to have written," he said, "My last books are too dry, I ought to have gone over them with a few layers of color, made my language precious in itself, like this little patch of yellow wall." Meanwhile he was not unconscious of the gravity of his condition. In a celestial pair of scales there appeared to him, weighing down one of the pans, his own life, while the other contained the little patch of wall so beautifully painting in yellow. He had rashly sacrificed the former to the latter."

Vermeer uses material to manipulate the viewer at a bodily level, and Proust does the same using his materials to evoke the sense of memory of past events. The long sentences and the relatively nonlinear sentence structure are more akin to the way memory and sense operate compared to previous novelists like Balzac or Flaubert. Relative to these, Proust's writing attains a formal aspect which, like Vermeer, is as much about the nature of perception as the telling of a story.

Provisional Conclusions

Vermeer's art practice is the result of the economic and social movement of the time. As stated, as Holland became more industrialized, particularly in the dye industry, there was great interest in the visual perception of color and color production. The huge scientific advancements in this area influenced Vermeer's practice. He knew Christian Huygens, one of the founders of modern optics, who visited him in his studio. He was also probably acquainted with Antony Van Leeuwenhoek (like Vermeer, also born in 1632 and from Delft), the physician who developed lenses and who was executor of Vermeer's estate. In Vermeer's work, the economic and social changes that spurred visual science came together with the communal elements still remaining in the guild system in Holland, where the division of labor was not yet in full force and where it was still socially encouraged to understand other crafts and disciplines as well as one's own. The contradiction of this situation produced results that cannot be explained by the narrative of Vermeer's work alone. They must also be explained as a physical effect brought about through the physical construction of the work by the artist.[3]

This chapter has tried to give an initial schematic of the way that these factors lead to works of visual art that combine intellectual knowledge with the skill of a manually and physically crafted object. The result is works that do not have the division of labor imprinted on them as an affect or an effect. The division that separates perception and the body into different "categories," as one way of upholding the dominant mode of production, is diminished. These works reveal by sensual means that this division is not "the way things are" or necessarily the way they are destined to remain.

2

Color, Facture, Art and Design

"The *forming* of the five senses is a labor of the entire history
of the world down to the present."

Karl Marx, *Economic and Philosophical Manuscripts of 1844*

"Painting was not figurative but represented nothing realistic:
it was a pictorial presence created by a painter who knew how
to specialize a surface to make it into a sort of highly sensitive
photographic plate destined not to photograph like a machine
but be present witness of the pictorial poetic moment; inspi-
ration, state of communication and enlightenment of the
artist, in the presence of all."

Yves Klein, *Long Live The Immaterial*

In Northern Europe since the late nineteenth century, synthetic
colors have been used profusely in the designed and built
environment. The majority of clothes, furnishings, cosmetics,
pharmaceuticals and many foods are dyed with one of a number
of hues that have emerged from industrial production. In the
modern industrial era there is great variety of color and theoretically the choice for the consumer has never been wider. This is
in sharp contrast to the time before Perkins' invented aniline
purple, when color was difficult and expensive to extract and the
luxury of coloring every synthetic object did not exist. Items
were left uncolored, or, usually they were gently dyed with one
of the relatively sparse available natural colorants. Natural dyes
often originated from Asia where for centuries they had been
extracted from diverse resources such as the cochineal insect,
madder root and lapis lazuli before being imported into Europe
for use by artists, ceramists, weavers and furniture makers. The

world at this time was very different to our present day with its multitude of durable synthetic colors, however, it can also be contended that some things have been lost in this process. Comparing modern day color production to that of the past, Delamare and Giuneau (2000) say:

"the very abundance of colors in the modern world seems to dilute our relationship with them. We are losing our intimate connection with the materiality of color, the attributes of color that excite all the senses, not just sight. Just as saffron yellow seems to have a certain scent and clay white to be soft and powdery to the touch all colors can be perceived according to their nature."

This chapter will argue that humans have such an intimate connection with the materiality of color and that in the modern environment this is lessened. Ultimately this is political and a major factor in the control and restriction of subjectivity at the level of the senses as it underpins dominant ideology. This latter idea originates from Marx's notion of the 'sensuous' which is touched on in his first thesis on Feuerbach:

"The chief defect of all hitherto existing materialism (that of Feuerbach included) is that the thing, reality, sensuousness, is conceived only in the form of the object or of contemplation, but not as sensuous human actively, practice, not subjectively. Hence, in contradistinction to materialism, the active side was developed abstractly by idealism, which, of course, does not know real, sensuous activity as such."

This was later explored more deeply in the *Economic and Philosophical Manuscripts of 1844*. The humanist/anti-humanist debate still rages around the *'1844 Manuscripts'*, based on its alleged connection to the transcendental legacy of European philosophy. The fact that the text pivots on a notion of human sensuousness in relation to the forces of production is often interpreted as the positing of the Absolute Spirit as a residue of Western bourgeois idealism. However, this has been disputed by Tedman (1999, 2004) who denies a division between the early 'humanist' and late 'scientific' Marx, partly on the grounds that the term 'sensuousness' should be translated from Marx's original German text of the manuscripts as 'sensual' and refer to the sensual bodily feeling of the species. Tedman also argues that Marx's own use of the term "species-being" in this work alludes to a concept of sensuality that is not essential though is still subject to change according to the physical environment, through the much slower change of evolution. In this chapter I utilize the concept of a material sensuality to analyze the sensual affective aspect of color that is created by the industrial forces of production and used in the designed and built environment.

In my view, the application of color within the fine art tradition is a highly advanced instance of production for our "intimate senses" in contrast with the modern industrial order of synthetic color. This conclusion is based on research that has been incorporated in an art historical study of the methods and techniques of a number of painters including Vermeer, El Greco, Rubens, Poussin, Turner, Uccello and Van Eyck. These disparate artists have in common an in-depth training with regard to art materials. With the exception of Turner, they were all educated within the rigors the guild system which entailed at least seven years familiarization with the vast body of knowledge comprising art materials and techniques. As a result, each of these artists were able to evolve specific methods and techniques and to construct unique combinations of materials. These materials were manipulated to serve their meticulous aims to create a distinctive affect, effect, feel and texture. The sources and utilization of the materials used in these works reflect the evolution of the "intimate senses" as an evolved sphere of perception manifested in the ability to respond with discernment to a wide range of textures, shapes and colors.

In this chapter I concentrate on the visual apparatus, conceived as a biophysical faculty that interacts with and informs all the senses, as an integral part of perception and contemplate some recent developments in psychology and physiology. The profound effect/affect of artistic color production is then compared with color produced in a modern industrial setting with the focus on the chemical components of the two largest synthetic color groups that dominate our environment today, the azo pigments and the pthalocyanines pigments. The omnipotence of these in the human environment are the result of economic pressures from the large cartels who produce the chemicals that make these colors. These chemicals are the by-products of other areas of the cartel's business - usually oil or coal - and the promotion and marketing of them increases the profitability of these companies.

I conclude the historical study of artistic technology by moving to the modern industrial period to examine an artist who used twentieth century technology to develop his artistic production specifically in contrast to the mass produced synthetic industrial color made under the economic restrictions of the oil-coal cartels. Yves Klein working with the chemist Edouard Adam used modern industrial processes to create synthetic colors and resin binders outside of the direct economic pressures of cartel production and as a result achieved sharply contrasting perceptual and aesthetic outcomes.

Art and Design:

Color Production and Art

What therefore are the possibilities of an "intimate connection" with color as Guineau and Delamare say? Within the visual arts (I concentrate mainly on painting) there are a number of professionals who to some degree reject the ordinary world to create their own environments. Their art-works are characterized by the huge amount of time and endeavor invested in learning how to arrange substances to affect the viewer. They developed and experimented specifically within the visual field on a daily basis to arrange matter as they would like it to be. The matter they arrange is the artist's materials. Some artists take this approach to an extreme and have distinct and even peculiar ways of organizing their materials to match exactly what they have discovered. This can be verified through observation of the working methods of artists. Turner for example spent many years and went to great lengths developing his late technique of thick white ground overlaid by thin paint layers containing a variety of media, wax, resin and oils. Poussin, Vermeer and El Greco also developed unique techniques for paint and ground. By using and developing various materials, each of these painters created artworks that interact with the visual capacities of the viewer to make a *specific sensory environment*. There are a number of materials available to artists to obtain this; pigments, binders, fillers and mixers, a variety of oils, resins, and waxes that are yielded from very many sources in nature.

In order to understand the artist's relationship with materials it is necessary to comprehend the wide range of sources at their disposal. The following, taken from Doerner's book *The Materials of the Artist* (1970), is a schematic list of substances that can be used to make paint, ground and varnish; cologne glue, bone glues, Russian glue, rabbit glue, gelatin and chalks, such as; marble white, Paris white, whiting, gypsum, kaolin, heavy spar, marble dust, pumice, stone powder, soapstone, zinc white, titanium white, lithopare and cremnitz white. A number of oils can also be utilized; cold pressed linseed oil, hot-pressed linseed oil, sun thickened oil, stand oil, oxidized oils, siccatif de Haarlem, Siccatif de Courtai, malbutter, nut oil, poppy oil, hemp oil, sunflower oil, soy bean oil, cottonseed oil, oil of turpentine and many more.

Natural color too, yields many sources for artists. The earth's crust contains numerous iron oxides, ochres and rubefied earths such as iron oxide rock. Iron oxide is initially black but depending on the size of the pulverized grams it produces shades ranging from violet-purple (0.5 microns) to red (0.1 microns) to orange (0.05 microns). Ochres also have many hues from yellow to red depending on the mixture of their composition of quartz sand, clay (kaolin) and iron oxide. Limonite, composed of goethite and poorly crystallized gels, produces a variety of yellows, as do plants such as Buckthorn berries and saffron. Mulberry juice yields red and purple and a variety of reds are derived from the herb, alkanet. Further red and purple pigments such as indigo, kermers and cochineal red come from a type of beetle and also from ardil, a red producing lichen which was originally used by Egyptian dyers. Further sources of red are aragonite, malachite, realgar and cinnabar vermilion which originates from mercury. Green pigments tend to come from rocks rich in green clay; glauconite, celadonites, chlorite. Greens are also made from copper salts. Chalk is used in the fabrication of some of the most widely used artists' white pigments, including the poisonous substance white lead. The list of the possibilities regarding pigments is partial and could be much longer.

This extensive number of pigments can be combined with the various resins, waxes and oils and so forth, in innumerable ways, creating the possibility of a huge number of grounds, pigments and varnishes each with their own particular visual and tactile characteristics. Depending on the substances chosen, the amount of each substance and how they are blended they can yield numerous, countless in fact, surfaces, tones and textures. The combination of materials used generatively to convey color and the affect they have on the canvas is known by the term 'facture.'

Chemistry: Vision and the Physical

What reference do artistic methods and the use of materials have to visual perception? Vision is usually meant as light-mediated information conveyed to the brain from the outside world. The conventional understanding, however, tends to ignore the link between the visual sense and the rest of the body. Recent developments in neurophysiology have established that the nervous system is so astutely integrated that the visual apparatus can inform the whole organism, on psychological as well as somatic levels. The effects are intricate, subtle and often function unconsciously. It is now recognized that the optic nerve splits into many different streams as it approaches the visual cortex. Some of these streams go to different parts of the brain and actually bypass visual consciousness to provide unconscious information to cognitive facilities other than vision. This in turn helps to guide behavior. This ability has been observed in blind subjects and has been labeled by the term *blindsight*. A study of conventionally blind subjects (whose primary visual cortex had been damaged or destroyed) revealed, for example, the ability to discriminate the position and even shape of light stimuli with near perfect accuracy (Azzopardi and Cowey 1997). These patients insisted they could not "see" or "feel" anything and that they were merely "guessing" where the light source was, thereby implying that visual neurological pathways still actively "perceiving" the light do not return to the visual cortex but to other parts of the body. These were possibly providing unconscious information or "intuition" as to the location of the light source. It was also discovered that a number of sighted subjects were correctly able to detect minute changes in computer images flashed at them without being able to define "rationally" what the changes were, they just 'sensed' the images were different. It was concluded that the visual system sent the relevant information to various parts of the body to produce a "gut feeling" and subjects could sense something had changed even if they did not know 'mentally' what that change was. (Rensink 2004).

The interchangeable relationship between the senses of touch and vision was demonstrated when normal-sighted subjects were blind-folded for several days and taught Braille. At first brain scans revealed total inactivity of the visual cortex but surprisingly, after a few days even with blindfolds, the cortex began to be activated again. The conclusion was that the cortex was being recruited by the brain to aid the subjects' touch sensation, *not* their visual sensation, for the purpose of learning Braille. What astounded scientists was how quickly the brain seemed able to utilize the visual cortex for this. The response was far too swift to be the result of the formation of completely new connections, so the investigators concluded that "tactile and auditory input into the "visual cortex" is present in all of us and can be unmasked if behaviorally desirable." The Applied Vision Research Center, London, states that recent studies show that contrary to previous supposition the pupil constricts in a systematic manner to stimulus such as spatial structure, color and movement, even when there is no change in the light flux. These stimuli are associated with the electrophysiological activity of neurons that do not return to the visual center of the brain but to other centers. The possibility arises of vision as but one sentient tentacle feeding information and feelings to the whole, and with the body adjusting itself to accommodate this in a much more mutable, economical and pragmatic sense than has previously been conceptualized. The senses can be seen to meld into each other with the distinction between one and the other - and the whole of cognition - not separate but to some extent interchangeable, almost topological.

Sarnat and Netsky's book (1981) on the evolution of the nervous system is based on Darwin's theory of evolution, tracing its development from an anatomical perspective. As they imply, the development and interaction of the hand has aided perception and allowed more intricate recognition of objects by texture, weight, shape and wetness. The practical use of the hand as coordinated with vision was as Engels accurately preempted:

"the most essential stimuli under the influence of which the brain of the ape gradually changed to man...along with the development of the brain came development of the senses."

It seems that the ability to discern between the massive variety of foliage and minerals in the environment to "understand the habits and anatomic vulnerability of hunted animals, and develop coordination of extremities and eye against moving targets" as well as to scan areas for safety created the necessity for a highly perceptive visual ability linked and integrated with the other senses. "As organisms became more complex, each new sensory capacity had to be integrated centrally with the other sensations." The result of this has been the development of the nervous system's multi-sensory capacities. One can comprehend how these abilities and recognitions are primal, often happening on levels that are very hard to verbalize, rationalize or even be conscious of. For this reason philosophy, poetry and literature are often the most successful examples for conveying these insights. For some writers, notably William Blake, D.H. Lawrence and Baudelaire, the formal arrangement of their language along with the imagery, successfully expresses the interconnecting nature of the senses as does an artist's formal arrangement of art materials and color in the facture of a painting. The poetic/prose arrangement operates therefore as facture in language.

The intricate subtlety of this highly developed aspect of cognition is lent further dimension by Hering's psycho-physio-logical prognosis of vision (Hering 1932) in contrast to Young/Helmholtz's emphasis on a chemical-based theory. In Hering's concept there are several parts to the perception of color; the source of the light, the chemical nature of the object that interacts with the light, and the eye and its receptors. Color is totally integrated and dependent on what materials light waves fall on and by the distinct way that the waves are affected by them. This phenomena is itself differentiated into three distinct categories; the *absorption* of some light wavelengths and the reflection of others; iridescence or *diffraction*, where contrasting wavelengths collide to create color and shapes; and, finally, *diffusion*, the effect of light passing through a prism for example. Accordingly, it is possible to perceive of color perception as entirely integrated with the physical nature of the material substance that creates the color and the enormous possibility of both obvious and subtle variations within this. In this sense there are as many different types of perceptible color as there are perceptible substances.

In view of how perception incorporates facilities like mindsight and blindsight it is possible to understand how infinitesimal changes in the construction of art materials can be observed and detected and can affect the body as a complete physical mechanism. Slight changes in the amount of specific resins, the use of one material underneath another, and tiny changes in mixing components are all discernible and detectable as different colors, textures and effects. As noted earlier, this use of materials can and has been made into the main subject matter of some works of art by certain artists who follow this path. The subtlety and variety of color and texture perceivable from the natural environment is reflected in the variety and specific combination of art materials used in these artworks. In their choices artists have at their disposal all of the discrimination and intricacy of the development of human perception through evolution and all its physical/visual reactions to the plethora of matter in the environment. Artists combine this knowledge with succinct use of the physical mechanisms of perception through color relations in order to locate and stimulate these facilities within the body. This is why some artists experiment for years to find specific combinations of ground and paint using the materials available to them and sometimes even when they are not easily available to them. From Italian Renaissance painters such as Duccio and Uccello, through to twentieth century masters like Popova and Mondrian, the history of art has many examples of artists who have followed this course.

Industrial Production and Color in the Built Environment

Organic synthetic dyes such as coal-tar dyes are today the main source of colored material in the environment. About half of these dyestuffs made are used for printing and graphic inks, a quarter are for architectural paints, and the rest for plastics, cements, ceramics, pharmaceuticals, cosmetics, food, automotive finishes, textiles and candles. Before the invention of synthetic dye in the nineteenth century, color in the designed and built environment usually came from more diverse and directly natural sources. It was often quite difficult and expensive to extract color and it required vast amounts of raw materials to make small quantities. By modern standards the range of dyes was limited and therefore color in man-made products was limited also. This began to change in the 1860s when Perkins extracted an artificial mauve dye using aniline or coal-tar which is a by-product of coal and oil processing. Over the next hundred years a number of industrialists seized on the opportunity that raw coal-tar offered and began to organize it into usable, saleable commodities. It attracted the attention of Carl Bosch of BASF, George Eastman at Kodak, E.I. Du Pont de Nemours of the company that bore his name. Color technology was also developed at companies such as Monsanto, Olin Corporation, the German cartel I.G. Farbens (*farben* means "colors" in German) whose subsidiaries have included BASF, Bayer, Hoechst and Agfa. These companies worked closely with the coal and oil companies that produced the raw coal-tar material, even sharing technology with them. In the USA, John D

Rockefeller's Standard Oil company shared technology with I.G. Farbens and in the 1930s and 1940s BASF, Bayer and Hoechst were all involved in petrochemical production in cooperation with Standard Oil. (The Esso brand name was created as a phonetic version of the initials SO, and Esso became the first foreign affiliate of Standard Oil.) Mergers were also common in the oil sector. In the 1950s Arco and Continental Oil were made into a subsidiary of the chemical manufacturer Du Pont and renamed Amoco and during the oil crisis of the 1970s Du Pont, by then a processing giant, took over the oil producer Conoco.

Oil producers have distilled great quantities of coal-tar raw material. By the 1940s this reached three million tons a year and today BP Petrochemicals alone sells 26 million tons annually. The fact that coal tar and other raw petrochemical materials are a by-product of oil production means that up until now there has been a plentiful and relatively inexpensive supply. This factor has enabled coal-tar dyes to be produced in vast quantities leading to the rapid growth of the synthetic dye industry in the nineteenth and twentieth centuries, when it gradually surpassed colors produced from natural dyes. A mere fifty years after Perkin's first invented aniline purple, there were over 2,000 synthetic colors, the presence of which hampered and ceased the production of many natural dyes and pigments (Hartley 1970).

Recently mergers between oil companies have increased and some observers interpret this as preparation for the on-coming peak oil crisis. This is the prediction that world oil production has reached its peak and is now in decline and as the world's population increases, therefore, critically, oil production will decrease. The decline of oil and petrochemicals is tipped to have massive implications in their use as both a direct source of power and also in the oil derivatives industries. For the moment however, the capital investment in petroleum-based and industrially produced dyestuffs ensures that they will be around for the foreseeable future.

Chemistry of Synthetic Coal Tar Dyes

Synthetic organic pigments (coal tar dyes) are fabricated from five basic raw materials; benzene, toluene, xylene, naphthalene and anthracene, which are also known as the aromatic hydrocarbons. Chemically all of these substances contain one or more benzene ring, which is a structure of six carbon atoms connected by delocalised electrons. These raw materials are first converted to compounds known as intermediates. One of the great number of intermediates is aniline which is made by replacing the hydrogen atom in one corner of the benzene ring with an amino acid (NH2), and phenol which is created by replacing one corner of the ring with a hydroxyl hydrogen atom. Various dyes and pigments are then created by combining these intermediates in various ways and from these few materials and processes a great variety of organic synthetic pigments are produced. The key to this lies in the chemical flexibility of carbon atoms, which can combine in a numerous variety of atomic structures, rings, chains and branches. These structures in turn can attach to other chemicals and to each other to produce many variations, including some that contain a large number of molecules with intense color attributes. Of these, the least toxic, most lightfast, and economical are manufactured as colorants.

Synthetic organic dyes and pigments may be classified into groups or families according to their molecular structure and the methods by which they are manufactured. The largest groups, the azo pigments, accounts for about 60 per cent of synthetic pigments and dyes and there are currently 336 manufactured. The azo pigments are created using the process of diazotization, which binds carbon into chains of six (benzene rings) and links them to complex chains with nitrogen and oxygen. Azo pigments can be made into any hue but they tend towards yellow, orange, red and brown. Another large class of pigments, phthalocyanines, create low cost blue and green colors and chemically have an affinity with the plant pigment chlorophyll (Ball 2001). This again involves a manipulation of four carbon rings linked by nitrogen, with the addition of chlorine to produce a greener or less green version.

The economic interest of industry for using these by-products has lead to the incorporation of dyes into all sorts of commodities, particularly pharmaceuticals and food, where their prime - and often only - function is 'cosmetic'. Fresh fruit is sometimes sprayed with synthetic dyes to even up the color, and they are ubiquitous in processed foods such as ice cream, jelly and tinned vegetables and the majority of cosmetics and toiletries. These artificial colors are known to cause a number of health problems in humans including allergies, as well as tumors in mice. Among the best known of these problematic chemical colorants are: E102 Tartrazine, E110 Sunset Yellow, E133 Brilliant Blue and E142 Green S. These have been linked to a variety of diseases, particularly among workers who have high exposures at their work place. As a result, great concern has arisen about the toxicity of these chemicals in recent years.

At a more fundamental level it is now known, for instance, that a synthetic estrogen is produced by some of these chemicals and that it mimics the natural hormone by attaching to estrogen receptors in the body. A number of health problems are now linked with this including infertility and some cancers. These xenoestrogens, as they are called, are found in hair dyes, cosmetics, plastics, hygiene products and pesticides and they are generally produced from petrochemical by-products. Two commonly used petrochemicals, benzene and xylene, which are also used in the process of making a number of synthetic colors, have particularly been singled out in relation to health problems. Among workers in occupations that come into regular contact with these toxins are; carpenters, auto mechanics, painters, commercial fishermen, furniture workers, dentists, electrical workers, potters, radiologists, staff in clothing and textile industries.

As a passing remark, this situation can be contrasted with the colorants of the pre-petrochemical era where the majority of substances such as those made from mulberry juice, alkanet, cochineal, ardil, ochres, gypsum, pumice, chalk, lime and natural resins extracted from tree bark, posed little or no health risk. There were, of course, some exceptions, such as chlorite, mercury, and lead, which are toxic. From as far back as the early twentieth century the industrial exposure of house painters to lead paint also meant that the average life span in this profession was eleven years shorter than the general population and both lead and cadmium may increase the risk of peripheral artery disease. In general, however, inherently toxic and ubiquitous synthetic coal dye products are difficult or impossible to avoid, and there is no control over their effects. By contrast the sheer variety of natural sources of paints and pigments makes it at least possible to avoid the use of cadmium and lead in paint in favor of less toxic substances.

Comparison of Production of Art Materials and Industrial Colors:
The Interdependence of Color and Form

To recapitulate, when light and color are perceived in nature it is through the various aspects of their structure i.e., what they are physically composed of. This factor plays a role in the visual perception of the vast variety of materials in nature inasmuch as color and structure are interdependent. That is to say, the atomic structure of the chemical components of a substance determines its color. It determines which light rays are reflected from it and which are absorbed or how intensely the light wavelengths combine or are split. The subtlety of this structural/textural/color relationship is manifest in the astute and integrated nature of the perceptual system which has evolved to be discerning on both rational and non-rational levels, since it involves intuition, feeling and sense.

However, in contrast to the diverse interaction of chemicals and substances that create color in nature, industrial synthetic color is largely reduced to five basic raw materials, all aromatic carbons, each of which is chemically based on the carbon benzene ring. More specifically, in the case of the widest category of synthetic pigments, the azo pigments, color production is based on reactions between benzene rings, nitrogen and oxygen. In the case of the other widely used group, the phthalocyanines pigments, it is based on a reaction between the benzene ring and chlorophyll. Synthetic color dyes are strong and uniform in color and they are used to color objects and materials, plastics, woods and metals. In other words synthetic colors *are added to the object from the outside* without any of the subtle integration of color with the substance of the object. The color is radically divorced from the structure of the physical object.

The present common notion of the quality of color, judged by its strength and its 'shining out' independent of its physical structure, is based on the proliferation of coal tar dyes. This is the tendency to divorce color from the physical effect of the structure and forms that it takes. It even permeates the thinking of scientists. When physiologists say we can see about 200,000 colors this disregards color as a physical medium that interacts with the structure that forms the color. The green of a plant and the green of a rock may measure up as exactly the same colors in terms of hue and saturation, but this does not mean they are the same color or even look the same because their chemical/physical components, the vehicles for the color, are different. This is often disregarded by the makers of synthetic color. As Ball (2001) says, even when scientists manage to reproduce molecules such as indigo and alizarin color synthetically, without any recourse to the raw material, they were keen not to differentiate:

"They had no qualms about naming a new pigment after its classical equivalent, as if deciding that 'Indian yellow' 'vermilion' and 'cobalt blue' designate not a substance but a hue."

It is possible, however, to make a virtually infinite combination of materials using the synthetic raw materials of carbon atoms. This in itself would make the color yielded from coal tar color much wider than it is, but it is limited by commerce. Coal tar and plastic producers have worked together in groups and cartels to establish the dominance of coal-tar pigments and dyes in the designed environment. The competitive nature of this has minimized and limited the type of product to large classes of pigments such as azo, which are the most economical to produce. This then is the political nature of design and color production as a sensual affect that is bound to have many repercussions on other areas of cognition. With the subtle relationship of the substance to the color removed and its replacement by an external source with limited facture, the color no longer stimulates the senses as evolved to perceive it.

Modern Contradictions of this in Art: Yves Klein

Yves Klein used the industrial technology of color to produce artworks. This was possible because Klein was able to stand outside the standard capitalist relations of color production and transform them according to artistic practice. As an artist he was removed from the direct pressures of mainstream industry in monopoly and cartel competition. To achieve this took a great deal of work concerning materials. Klein's initiation with industrial methods was a long and technically rigorous process that began for him as an exploration of the production of art in all its physical aspects. He worked as a

picture framer in London and, "It was there, while working on the preparation of glues, colors and varnishes, gilding...that I got closer to materials" (Klein 2000). Klein later began to manufacture his own pigments, working in conjunction with the chemist, Edouard Adam. Together they experimented for a year by manipulating the coal-tar process that produces synthetic ultramarine pigment to make a blue pigment with a specific chroma. This was eventually registered under an international patent and named International Klein Blue, often referred to as IKB. The next stage was to develop a resin that would enable this pigment to stick to various surfaces while maintaining its dusty powdery effect and "without diluting the color". As a result of their success in developing a resin with these characteristics, an original technical development in painting, the surface of the resulting paintings are almost solely composed of the primary chemical substance that makes the color: the pigment. With the development of the resin binder, Klein attempted to minimize interference with the intensity of the color.

In these works, known as the IKB series, color emanates from the physical object as opposed to being added from the outside as in the case of commodities bearing synthetic color. The artist has manipulated the medium to directly link to the surface of the object; the result is that the IKB series of works are visually or sensually quite shocking as the rarity of the colored surface immediately becomes apparent to the viewer by its brilliance, intensity and physical affect. By creating their own pigment and binder Klein/Adam thus demonstrate a shift in the economically pre-determined circumstances controlling this field as they intervene in the mass production of coal-tar dyes and their proliferation in 'everyday' life. Klein's quest to intervene in this process can be compared to some of his contemporaries. In my opinion, for instance, while Warhol's ironic stance to some extent demystifies art and reveals the technique of the printing process, it also heralds popular culture and mass production through its subject matter and its means of production in what he called "The Factory". Compared to Klein's extreme measures, Warhol also conforms to a more conventional use of industrially mass produced artists' materials in many of his works. For example, in the *Campbell's Soup Can* series, Warhol uses artists' quality acrylics, and printing inks.

One cannot easily produce all of the objects in everyday life with the skill of a work of art. The few artists who specialize in color and facture in relation to the senses as their full-time occupation stand in contrast to the industrial producers who do not have the economic facility to incorporate this objective as a primary factor. The contrast between the ordinary everyday industrial world and certain kinds of *extraordinary* artistic production gives such art a rare quality. Art that targets human perception in this fuller sense as its main criteria is very unusual. What is, in fact, the very skilled use of materials on the part of the artist starts to seem incredible, when the materials manifest into a rare creation that, as its prime object, heralds the human faculty.

The work of Yves Klein is, as a result, harnessed as an ideological referent for color in art as transcendentally detached from its physical component. Klein is often represented as the painter of "the void", who attempted to express color in its metaphysical or non-physical state. This persisted in the Hayward Gallery London exhibition of 1995 which was entitled *Into The Void*, and continues to exist in the majority of printed matter about Klein, although discussion of the lengthy and extremely rigorous technical aspects of his practice are usually omitted. The metaphysical quality of Klein's work is also noted in the comments that accompany his work in museums and galleries. For example, Jasper Morrison's statement next to Klein's blue painting *IKB79* (1959) on the wall at the Tate Modern Gallery in London claims, "like all great works it is beautiful beyond physical beauty..." and also says that Klein wished to make painting immaterial and "beyond the visible or tactile."

Yet, the artist's manipulation of the pigment so that it is directly integrated with the physical surface of the object and the affect of this on the "materiality of the senses" makes Klein's art precisely *not* transcendental or spiritual. The direct integration of the color into the physical surface of the object means that it is more intrinsic to the object and not transcendent from it. In addition, the integrated physical nature of the work as the result of industrial techniques was produced in economic dissociation from the forces that control the struggle for dominance between cartels. Klein manifests, therefore, a form of practice which has become relatively liberated from mainstream capitalist forces of production. The transcendental emphasis given to this by the art establishment is an ideological marker that obfuscates this aspect and impedes the radical elements of the work.

Some Conclusions

While the natural world evolves an enormous variety of perceptual experience through its interaction with the visual system, synthetic production reduces this to a highly limited number of materials and processes. Use of these strong, lightfast and inexpensive synthetic colors are at the expense of nuance, tincture and the plenitude of the natural formation. Consequently, the body in the built environment is presented by synthetic materials with a limited amount of facture and subtlety compared to what it is physically capable of perceiving. Synthetic color has its own physical components, of course, but these are still separate from the physical nature of the objects that it colors. Thus, color and its perception become detached from the physical nature of the object and factors such as brightness, color-fastness and cost effectiveness take precedence. The body's appropriation of the physical aspect of color and beyond that, the materiality and physical effect of nature itself is channeled into passively observing color divorced from structure. The perception of color becomes separated from the relationship between materials and structure and the intricacies of this relationship on related cognitive-processes.

A history of criticism of this state of affairs is implicit in the work of a number of theorists.

In the *1844 Manuscripts* Marx says that under capitalism the process of proletarian labor is separate or:

> "is external to the worker i.e., it does not belong to his intrinsic nature; that in his work, therefore, he does not affirm himself but denies himself, does not feel content but unhappy, does not develop freely his physical and mental energy but mortifies his body and ruins his mind."

More specifically on the aspect of synthetic color production and its use, in 1883 William Morris said:

> "I want modern science, which I believe to be capable of overcoming all material difficulties, to turn from such prepos-

terous follies as the invention of anthracene colors."

As we have observed, anathracene is one of the five aromatic hydrocarbons that enter into the manufacture of coal tar colors. Morris considers it to the one aspect of the "the cheap and nasty wares which are the mainstay of competitive commerce, and are indeed slave-wares, made by and for slaves."

A method for analyzing the effect of this lies in Tedman's thesis, which adds another, aesthetic level to the base/super-structure model at the core of the Marxian critique of political economy and culture. Tedman (1999) states:

> "The authentic subject is the human subject as a member of a species that produces objects that confirm the humanness of the senses as they have evolved as a species, and not as the capitalist economic, conventional relations have enforced. Because all objects produced by labor are, under these exploitative conditions and circumstances, felt to be both these things - alien objects that estrange and confirmation of an authentic subject - it still remains just possible for a bitter-sweet pleasure to be experienced through labor. Again we must emphasize that this authentic subject itself is not fixed for all time (evolution takes care of that), but neither does it change with every change of conventional economic relations."

The ubiquitous nature of coal-tar colors makes them the prime representative of color in the designed and built environment. As such they are one of the prime sources for the confirmation of the potential of the body's response to color in its multi-sensory aspect and in the affectation of feeling.

In the workplace, labor under capitalism, is alienation for the worker, but it is also necessary and affirms the senses of the worker. At the level of consumption, objects colored with coal-tar dyes, are both necessary as part of the affirmation of the senses of the worker and also alienating to the senses. As commodities they provide responses that solidify estrangement at the level of consumption. As color and its perception becomes detached from the physical nature of the object, a vital aspect of the connection with nature is channeled into observing color divorced from structure. Color presented in this limited form may be inexpensive and practical but does not appeal to the body in a material sense. In other words, color as a physical structure that corresponds with the integrated structure of the body, as this has evolved, is not articulated. Instead, color is separated from the relationship between materials and structure. As the intricacies of these relationships are lost, so is the sensual ground of related cognitive processes. Color therefore seems to become a Cartesian abstraction separated from its material and physical components and the repercussions of this on the human subject. Objects of this kind in the designed environment promote a transcendent and spiritual metaphysic, and utilize feeling to underpin estrangement on the bodily, or aesthetic level. The emphasis is of mind over matter on the level of the senses and along with this, of the triumph of capital as an abstract force ruling over labor.

It can now be seen that the capitalist forces of production that Marx speaks of as destructive to the worker's sensual capacities are, as he implies, not confined to the workplace. The disregard for the subtleties of the worker's mind, emotions and body existing in the workplace also act on the products created under these conditions. The low cost, limited facture, limited color, limited processing and competition between large monopolies in the instance of coal-tar dyes are the prime forces that produce color with the same indifference for the consumerist senses and in the designed and built environment as the capitalist process has for the productive senses of the worker. In this particular means of production, these forces therefore become embodied in the use-values of those commodities in which color is embedded. The sensual affect of this color is one of disregard for sensual cognitive capacities. The facilities for perception and the development of the nervous system, the ability to perceive color relations, their facture, and their effect on the body characterized by the example of the phenomena of mindsight, blindsight, and in the work of artists, go unheeded.

Thus, the particular aspect of design in these circumstances neutralizes the sensual and perceptive potential of the subject. A different environment - one that took these facilities into account - would encourage even more articulated and subtle responses through the body, physically, mentally, creatively, giving rise to the possibility of much greater levels of invention and production and not to contain it to the use of the human 'machine,'.

Although Marx and Engels themselves did not write a great deal on the theme of art and color, there is peripheral evidence that they were quite conscious of its immediate effects, even specifically of the role of synthetic color. In 1868 when Engels undertook to note his *Confessions*, the popular Victorian pastime which involved filling out a questionnaire of personal tastes, he was asked what his favorite color was. To this he replied; *"any one not Aniline"*.

3

Visual Syntax

"It is the object itself and its internal working and internal contradictions that makes it exist at all, not just external things i.e. the human body is a material object and its mechanism for perception is as important a part as the external forces."

Mao Tse-Tung

"The life of the species, both in man and in animals, consists physically in the fact that man (like the animal) lives on organic nature; and the more universal man (or the animal) is, the more universal is the sphere of inorganic nature on which he lives. Just as plants, animals, stones, air, light, etceteras, constitute theoretically a part of human consciousness, partly as objects of natural science, partly as objects of art - his spiritual inorganic nature, spiritual nourishment which he must first prepare to make palatable and digestible - so also in the realm of practice they constitute a part of human life and human activity. Physically man lives only on these products of nature, whether they appear in the form of food, heating, clothes, a dwelling, etceteras. The universality of man appears in practice precisely in the universality which makes all nature his inorganic body both inasmuch as nature is (1) his direct means of life, and (2) the material, the object, and the instrument of his life activity. Nature is man's inorganic body - nature, that is, insofar as it is not itself human body. Man lives on nature, meaning that nature is his body, with which he must remain in continuous interchange if he is not to die. That man's physical and spiritual life is linked to nature means simply that nature is linked to itself, for man is a part of nature."

Karl Marx *1844 Economic and Philosophical Manuscripts*

Marx confirmed that the humanities and arts were in fact sciences. Philosophy, history and ideology were rendered scientific by describing their relationship to the economic base which is the material connection of these subjects to the world beyond thought. The specific location of art, however, within this schema is still notoriously contentious.

In art practice the role of the base is visible when the raw materials of artistic production derived from nature, the art materials, are transformed by labor to fulfill their use value. The crucial use-value of art is its value to the sensuality of the subject and this is its essential powering element. There are few other industries or professions with this particular remit. The artistic profession contradicts other modern industries which have elements such as efficiency, practical utility, speed of production, cost effectiveness and profit as their fundamental basis.

As stated already, the specifics of the role of art in its material relation to the base can be located by the concept of an aesthetic level of practice (Tedman 1999). This aesthetic construes the concept of species-being from Marx's *1844 Manuscripts* as non-humanist, material and sensual and is based on the psycho-physiological construction of the body. It describes the traffic between base and superstructure and between the levels from the point of view of human sensuality, feeling and the body. With the motor of sensual labor-power at its core the aesthetic level provides a materialist methodology that situates art, a sense-based discipline, in perspective to the material base, thus forging its relationship to science and therefore to other scientific disciplines. The scientificization of art enables a clear view of its location next to established cognitive scientific subjects such as language, mathematics, anthropology, physiology and politics.

I think that Uccello is one example of an artist who selected materials from the natural environment and presented them in the work of art in a distilled and intensified fashion especially in order to stimulate the sensory nature of the whole perceptive body to fulfill the use-value of art. Briefly this comprises of an unearthing of the subtleties of our senses which were formed via responses to the plethora of matter in the natural world, of the subtle complexity of substances and their colors. To this end the artist has combined selectively chosen matter from the natural world, the art materials, to stimulate vision to extend or fulfill its sensitive sensual potential, not only affecting vision, I think, but the whole body. This is to some extent manipulating the human response to nature but in an organized fashion which condenses and intensifies it, perhaps even more than the natural environment. Based on the success of this hypothesis Uccello has produced "masterpieces".

The concept of syntax will here explore the secular nature of this process of attainment of the artistic use-value. The term is used in the Chomskian sense as a set of natural abstract structures and faculties. It confirms the scientific nature of art by its sense connection to the physical material base and also to related fields such as language, mathematics, physiology and the physics of color. We examine these disciplines in search of a point of intersection between them where resides the platform to describe the holistic nature of art as it impacts the whole body as a rational thinking and also feeling entity.[4] In this chapter the probing of linguistics as the basis for a syntactic theory of visual perception uses Saussure's original argument of the distinction between the arbitrary and the associative elements, the latter of which he labeled the "innerstorehouse" and "langue". The influence of this to Chomsky's notion of deep structure as a physical capacity (1980) originated the concept of syntax in language. The physical nature of which is in this chapter edified by Freud's conjectures into the evolution of the simple primitive organism as part of the holistic development of both the psyche and the physical body. These sources merge with the biological phenomena of neural adaptation and its manifestation in vision; color after-image, to confirm the corporeal basis of rational perception and its relevance to vision. Thus elucidating the organized nature of syntax in art as a non-arbitrary formalization of intrinsic sensual properties, the manipulation of which is apparent in the painting by Paolo Uccello *Nicolo di Maruzi da Tolentino at the Battle of San Romano.*

I will conjecture that the technical definition of the term syntax in art has both surface structure, the arbitrary aspect, as well as a deep structure which takes the form of color relationships. This is particularly notable in some artistic presentations where the arbitrary element is minimized in favor of the deep structure of systematic color sensuality. It is also an indication of exactly how the perception of art, most particularly via some art objects, is distinct from language or mathematics which have more prominent arbitrary elements.

The use and comparison of art to other cognitive phenomena is not particularly new or contemporary. Poussin,[5] Turner and Mondrian for example, each had their own conception of systematic and organized relationships between their work with other, at first seemingly disparate, physical and cognitive disciplines and faculties. The contemporary use of the specific term *syntax* however comes to art from the theory and practice of the systems painter Jefferey Steele. Steele is intrigued by the Chomskian notion of deep syntactic linguistic structures and their application to the visual arts. As a painter Steele is directly influenced by the formalist artists of the Soviet avant-garde and also Mondrian, Max Bill, Richard Lohse and Kenneth and Mary Martin and in turn has himself inspired a number of contemporary systematic artists.

A Note Concerning Perspective

This chapter primarily concerns color, its substance and the forms these take in the work of art. To achieve this it then omits much reference to other qualities in painting such as the figurative and symbolism and also the scientific and perceptual basis for perspective. As a result, diminishing viewpoints, central focus and other features that are derived from the capabilities of real vision to form perspective in paintings are minimally detailed.

Parallels With Linguistics:
Simple syntactic origins in Saussure; the arbitrary element in language

In linguistic studies Chomsky explains syntax as thus;

Phonetic and the Semantic
Brought together in
Language through a set of abstract natural structures.
These are called Syntactic Structures

As we said the origins of syntax in language in the modern era comes from Saussure who stated that:

"the linguistic sign is arbitrary. The idea of "sister" is not linked by any inner relationship to the succession of sounds s-o-r which is its signifier in French, that it could be represented equally well by just any other sequence is proved by differences amongst languages and by the very existence of different languages." (Ferdinand de Saussure, *Course in General Linguistics*)

As he infers, there are more and less arbitrary systems of signification. The subject is stimulated by the direct sensual impact of their environment, and the basic senses of sound, sight, touch, smell and taste are the receptors for this. Most infants enter the world with all of these intact but unable to talk, which is learnt later. Language, of course, did not spontaneously manifest, it has a history and has not always existed in its present form. The arbitrary aspect of language is a reflection of the variations and changes of it throughout history. This form can be studied at any period, but according to Saussure the *changing temporal aspect* of language, the diachronic, must be disregarded in order to study the form. In the study of language therefore the diachronic temporal element is distinguished from the synchronic, *spatial mechanism,* such as:

"Everything that relates to the static side of our science is synchronic; everything that has to do with evolution is diachronic. Similarly, synchronic and diachronic designate respectively a language-state and an evolutionary phase."[6]

Saussure explains that the co-ordinations formed inside discourse are the single words which are learnt by the speaker. These are morphological and derive from convention until they become associative. The associative part is the "inner storehouse" and refers to the spatial and non-linear mechanism of linguistic order.[7]

The classification and analysis of these categories preludes transformational generative grammar which itself is a theorization of the status and distinction between the arbitrary and associative elements. It is based on Saussure's theory that meanings of words are conventional and isolated when not examined in the context of the associative. Chomsky's addition of the term 'deep structure' was founded by an examination of various languages (and also anticipated for others) to develop very basic rules that govern them. Deep structure takes the form of kernel sentences, present in all languages (therefore re-named

Universal Grammar), and is considered part of a sensual and physical creative facility. This is proved by the infinite number of completely new sentences generated by people every day and the fact that every one of these can be "felt" to be correct or not.[8] According to Chomsky the sound or phonetic element is linear and the structure used to encode it is also linear, but the structure used to encode the meaning is not linear but multi-dimensional and spatial, such as Saussure's synchronic component.

Relationship of Mathematics and Natural Language

As modes of communications both mathematics and natural language both consist of deep structure and also surface structure. Both represent information the mind can facilitate and systematize, provided that the arbitrary symbolic meanings are already understood.

Mathematics, like natural language, consists of symbolic notations which refer to elements, compounds and the outcome of their interaction. The expression of these transactions reach human sensibility in the form of arbitrary symbolism, or, surface structure, integrated with and giving rise to non-arbitrary deep structure as the *sense* that these are correct or not.

The symbols used in mathematics are shorter and more condensed than those applied in language. Pure mathematics can be said to be an ideal form of syntax. It does not refer to things 'in the world' only to itself. As the working mind "performs" mathematics it bears reference to the mode of the relationships that the mind is able to acknowledge and use. Mathematics is an unraveling of comprehensible methods and the transcription of logic. As Quine (1964) says:

"pure mathematics [is] unlike physics in being quite independent of observation and experiment."

Mathematics features in so many cognitive disciplines, because these disciplines are as much about describing mental and sense application as about the subjects being dealt with. They enable existing phenomena to become appropriated by human consciousness as a sensual yet non-anarchistic interpretation.

As we said about language, mathematics too is *felt* to be *correct* or *not* in its rational and logical countenance. This is because the rational and mental elements present in mathematics and also language originally evolved physically from the mutation and natural selection of very simple organisms. In Freud's *Beyond the Pleasure Principle* this early development is articulated as the biological origin of the psyche. Freud was Lamarckian, so it is possible to interpret his ideas on the development of the organism as the inheritance of acquired characteristics but they can also be easily understood in the context of Darwinian evolution. Freud explains the very simple homogenous and featureless organism, rather like an amoeba perhaps, in its advance from a formless mass towards the sentient and topographical "special arrangement" of the senses:

"This little fragment of living substance is suspended in the middle of an external world charged with the most powerful energies; and it would be killed by the stimulation emanating from these if it were not provided with a protective shield against stimuli. It acquires the shield in this way: its outermost surface ceases to have the structure proper to living matter, becomes to some degree inorganic and thenceforward functions as a special envelope or membrane resistant to stimuli."[9]

The protection against stimuli is very important for the living organism, almost as important as the reception of stimuli. This partly inorganic shield preserves the organism and its "special modes of transformation" from the enormously harsh effects of the environment, which could "level out these energies" and bring about their destruction. The senses are the "receptive cortical layers" which "in more highly developed organisms have sunk into the protective interior of the body with sensitive portions of it remaining on the surface."

The body is perceived as an integrated mechanism with its internal own structure for processing exterior forces. It can be speculated that as sensory and cerebral evolution progressed and each of the surface senses became specialized, beneath the "receptive cortical layers" the interior of the body continued to function in an integrated fashion to some extent. The inner layers retain both their sensitivity and the homogenous character of a centralized nervous system even through the later stages of development of consciousness and rationalism. The organism remains therefore a spatial entity consisting of an internal mélange with the senses left "behind on the surface" with their own "special arrangements".

Freud's biological perspective of the evolution of the psyche and rationalism is in contradistinction to classic Western philosophers such as Descartes where the "seat" of thought is in the head, connoting transcendence and a-priori knowledge. Likewise in the contemporary era the integrated nature of the senses initially described by Freud have become subject to intense investigation. Many scientific experiments have demonstrated the relationship between vision and other senses. It has been shown for example that nerve impulses from the visual cortex are able to rapidly re-route in order to aid other senses, such as touch, evidencing that the physical capacity, "the pathways" to do this already exist. (See (Rensink 2004) (Azzopardi, Cowey et al. 1997) (Marchant 1992) and for a fuller discussion see Chapter 2.)

The Nature of this Mediative Organization

The contemporary evolution of the arrangement of internal sensory mediators with the external world as Freud describes, of how our bodies filter out and control the reception of a plethora of sensation, can be observed in the perception of hot and cold. The external environment yields temperature at widely varying levels that guarantee that hot and cold are never presented to the body in equal measure but fluctuate according to environment, climate and season. Yet, despite this, the perception of hot and cold has developed to function as an equilibrium within the body because the body organizes the sensations of hot and cold as balanced opponents. Numerous experiments with temperature demonstrate this, for example, when one hand is placed in hot water and the other in cold water and both hands then are put into tepid water, the hand from the hot water will feel cold and conversely the hand from the cold water will feel hot. This is because both heat and cold sensors each decline as they become overloaded with the hot or cold sensation therefore the perception of each of these sensations automatically switches to the opposite, even if the heat source in the external world remains the same. This organizational quality of perception is known as neural adaptation. Similar processes are known to occur throughout the body. In the case of auditory adaptation, for example, this manifests as a decline in the ear's response to sound.

The process of neural adaptation is known to affect all the senses of the body, as Stocker and Simoncelli (2009) purport, because adaptation is a ubiquitous characteristic of perception and the effects appear across all sensory modalities. Adaptation is in fact a fundamental property of biological sensory systems that are able to adapt their sensory behavior in response to the context of recent sensory experiences. They are a fundamental facility of the sensory system that operates throughout the body in the other senses; taste, smell and touch and in cognitive

74

perceptive facilities such as orientation, hand-eye co-ordination, motion after-affects and the perception of darkness and light and of color.

It must be reiterated that the use of the term adaptation is not to be confused with adaptation in the Lamarckian sense. Adaptation here refers to neurological characteristics formed through generations as long-term evolutionary processes. Perhaps a better term for neural adaptation in this non-Lamarckian context is something like sensual equilibrium because it refers to a mediating facility of the body in order for it to conciliate the external world. However the process does demonstrate how the "special arrangement" of the physical body works as an equilibrium or a reflex mechanism that uses oppositions to experience sensation.

Color

Sensual equilibrium (neural adaptation) as it functions in color perception can be confirmed by the ubiquitous presence of the color green in nature where the abundance of the chemical chlorophyll means that green is often more prolific than red in the environment. The unique chemical composition of each leaf or blade of grass stimulates the visual capacity to acknowledge very slight chromatic and tonal distinctions to yield very many shades of greenness. The distinguishing characteristics of these innumerable green shades, tones and colors are dependent on the amount and distribution of chlorophyll in each part of the plant, the time of day and the affect of shade. It could be construed that with the vast proliferation of green in nature and the acute sensitivity to perceive its many manifestations, that vision should have developed with more sensitivity towards green and less towards red. However this is not the case, the body has equal ability to see both red and green within its spectral field because these two colors function together through a visual version of sensual equilibrium (neural adaptation), which is known as after-image.

What is After-Image?

As a challenge to the tri-chromatic color theory of Young-Helmholtz, Ewald Hering theorized four basic colors that seem unique and function in opposition as red-green and yellow-blue. He noted these oppositions are antagonistic to each other and do not blend. As a result of this, when the eye is fixed on a given color and that color is removed, the sensation of seeing the original color remains for a brief period of time. This is known as the positive after-image and is followed quickly by the negative after-image. The negative after-image is always very nearly the same as the opposite of the original color; red and green replace one another and so do yellow and blue. This is called the opponent-process theory.[10] Hering stressed that these responses are not isolated, but that the entire visual system is interconnected, that a response in one nerve fiber could antagonize a nearby fiber and prevent it from responding to a stimulus. Hering describes the formal arrangement of color as discreet binary oppositions which are positive and negative just like the fundamental components of mathematics.

As well as describing the psycho-physiological element of vision Hering was equally keen to recognize the importance of the chemical aspect. He considered this was integrated with the physiology of vision as its chemical constituent because vision, as already noted, is equally dependent on the chemical composition of each of the material substances that rays of light fall on, as on *the light rays themselves* (the "physics" element). Depending on this chemistry the rays are altered accordingly and have a different effect on the visual cortex to make different colors. Thus emphasizing that color perception has evolved because of its relationship to both light and chemical substances and that it is synthesized by the multitude of physical compounds on the planet that are its material vehicles. Again, color has evolved therefore, to be integrated with form and substance. The thousands of plants, rocks, minerals, animals and other phenomena impart a diversity of color that, for human vision, is totally dependent on their material and chemical composition. We can once more refer to the color green and its many apparent incarnations. We see many types of green, all dependent on the exact chemical composition of a particular substance, of plants for example, as well as the time of day, the temperature, shade and our position in relation to this. *It demonstrates that our visual evolution is as much about understanding color as a substance, its vehicle, as well as the way the relationship between each color affects our eyes.*

I contest that some artists have explored the reciprocal attributes of the chemical substance of vision and the effect of this on the sensual body which includes rationality. The results of this are sometimes manifest in the work of artists on a holistic physical level that is both rational and sensual. We will now present how this attests to the potency of art as potentially the most purely aesthetic or sensual method of exploring and manipulating the organized nature of the mediation of the body with the external world. This is in part because unlike pure mathematics or language, art requires no arbitrary knowledge to "read" or "interpret" the sensual and syntactic relationship between colors. The presentation of color need contain no surface structure to have optimum affect. In this case a direct impact occurs upon the senses at the very moment of presentation.

We will give an example of how a work of art involves relationships that use the mathematical aspect of the abstract nature of the color system, though totally synthesized with the materials of the colors as they work throughout the whole visual apparatus. Speaking schematically this can be demonstrated in relationships of the red-green color binary within the Paolo Uccello painting *Niccolo Mauruzi da Tolentino at the Battle of San*

Romano. The overall affect of the painting is largely based on this and on other similar color relationships. If the eye focuses on the color green in the bushes that form the mid background of the painting, for example, the excitation of the green cone creates red as an after-image. This serves to heighten the colors containing red in the painting such as the oranges and the pink of the lower foreground. This process of color functioning in opposition continues as the cones and rods become saturated and are switched on and off. Put very simply, the green color creates a red afterimage that as its opposite therefore, visually cancels out the green. This lessens the intensity of the greenness in the painting while at the same time intensifying the colors that contain red. This saturation of redness from the painting in turn creates a green afterimage that weakens the perception of red and then again green and so forth. So the eye is in a constant state of stimulation and adjustment regarding color that, as Hering says, affects the whole system of color perception and vision. In the painting Uccello uses the oppositions of red/green and also blue/yellow and black/white to stimulate the visual organization of the fundamental mathematical constituents of positive and negative elements in visual perception.[11]

The painting is figurative but it has flat areas of paint to emphasize the relationships of color with a simple formality so I suggest the figurative element does not detract from the formal color relationships. The material construction of the colors also serves to embellish the visual significance of these relationships. For example, Uccello used walnut oil-tempera and linseed oil-tempera to make his paint. The chief characteristic of tempera is that it less shiny and less easy than oil paint to be "worked into" to make accurate copies of objects and to contrive perspective. Tempera therefore highlights the flat texture of the color/pigment and diminishes the shiny reflective surfaces that in other art works often contribute to the effect of receding illusion. In *The Battle of San Romano* the use of tempera along with the simple, formal areas of color accentuate the color relationships and the unctuous physical properties of the materials, such as the nutty texture of the sheen of walnut oil. This texture also exposes the lines of the grain of the wood panel still visible through the paint.

As I said earlier, the layer underneath the paint, the ground, is sited by Doerner to have a very potent affect on the color and texture of the paint surface. The ground used by Uccello is made from Plaster of Paris, also known as anhydrite or slightly burnt gypsum and also gypsum (hydrated calcium sulphate), gelatin, glue size and water (Roy 1997). When I mixed these ingredients to prepare a ground similar to the one used by Uccello it appeared quite thin when picked up on the brush and applied to the surface but then thickened as the gesso powder gathered in some areas of the surface. This made the ground slightly uneven so that the paint formed into little pools of varying intensity of color over the top of the ground. Despite these slight variations in color intensity, the overall effect of the painting is one of flatness. Technical nuances of this sort can be seen in the original painting. One is aware that Uccello has selected various items from the plethora of available materials in nature and combined them so that the ingredients have a bearing on each other. The different layers of ground and paint that he has chosen, interact with the pigments, oils and egg, and all of them combine and contrive to bring subtle sheens, colors and layers to the formally simple construction of the painting.

Uccello and other likeminded artists spend much time on the method of presentation of color. The manipulation of the material part of the painting, the art materials, is paramount in order to *oppose* the expression of color *as part of a non-tactile substance* and to express it as it is, formed by the collusion of the materials of the earth united with the somatic systematic relationships of vision. Age old sensibilities entwined in our evolution to discern millions of types of chemicals on the planet through their color and factural texture is the subject matter in art works such as this. These sensitivities form the most basic and extreme evolutionarily necessities and are therefore found in the most profound areas of perception. This aspect of Uccello's work forms the somatic formal organization that allows us to *feel* the truth whether in mathematics, in rational possibilities or in art. The rational and physical interior mélange of the early primitive organism and its advanced outreach components in the form of both thought and the senses are stimulated. This is unity of the *natural abstract binary structure* of color that parallels Chomsky's reference to linguistic syntax as a set of *natural abstract structures.*

The materials and construction of the painting are very important to artists such as Uccello, who want to expose the material nature of the relationships of color as part of a substance and thus to have the relationship of color to both the *abstract and to the physical* realizable.

Art is a point of conjunction between these elements; our relationship with physical matter and our relationship to abstract matter which includes the rational. Again, just as all scientific, linguistic or mathematical knowledge has to be *felt* to be true as well as rationally understood, what scientists and mathematicians call "the beautiful theory" follows through to art where the body, sense feeling and rational knowledge exist in their ability to utilize all these faculties as a unity. The "beauty" is in the stimulation and functioning of these relationships with the senses. It is the materialist aesthetic heightening of the senses. This is the *feeling* of physical facilities in contact/harmony with external elements in the world, the work of art specially derived for this purpose. A synchrony forged through the harmonized evolution of the body and external nature and pleasure is the functioning of this instrument in a complete sense.

As human ciphers, artists such as Uccello are aware of abstract and visceral relationships and target the visual mechanism in their painting, with the aim of exploiting these phenomena and setting them to work. In viewing the painting the subject is therefore looking at his or her own bodily facility, through the body of the artist, externalized onto an object. The legacy of this can be seen in the work of modern day system painters who have consciously extracted color oppositions as a vital part of their subject matter and minimized or attempted to totally negate the figurative element. These artists use color oppositions as proposed by Hering to stimulate physical facilities and sometimes employ numbers, algebra and group theory to calculate, construct and organize these relationships. However, even without this conscious pursuit most artists are aware of these relationships intuitively. Sensory equilibrium is therefore manipulated by various historically skilled artists and also some modern artists so that it functions at its most intense. Color and its media are extracted to appeal to the organization of the senses very succinctly. It is this most sensual physical and concentrated format that constitutes the effect of very sophisticated works of art on the mental and physical capacities of the viewer. It is the reason why art of this kind provides a unified heightening of the senses and rationale because as part of a holistic physical system sensual equilibrium permeates the whole physical being. In this aspect it functions primarily not on the level of ideology but on the aesthetic level, that of the senses and feeling. For these reasons Uccello's painting seems modern even though it is almost 600 years old.

As we have seen, the perception of color in art is derived from a visual syntax which differentiates from the syntax of language and mathematics because there is no necessity for an arbitrary element. The arbitrary element in perspective and the figurative nature of the paintings have, we have argued, less importance in perception at this level.

Of course a pure color in a painting can still be associated with something else, figurative elements outside of the painting. Bright red could be associated with a London bus for example. It may be very difficult for the viewer to avoid this association or others like it depending on their experience. However what we are referring to here in the work of selective artists is that color is presented as part of a system. The importance is the relationship *between* the colors, this relationship is not arbitrary, it competes and even overwhelms any arbitrary signification. The history of art as a disciple, however, often emphasizes the symbolic, personal memory and figurative aspects of art and there is not much emphasis on the physical components and their relationship at this level.[12] As we shall see the significance of this level of visual perception and its connected somatic faculties cannot be underestimated in the comprehension of art and culture.

4

Women, Culture, Class, Labor

"The woman who bears the trials and tribulations of recon-
structing the economy on an equal footing with the man, and
who participated in the civil war, has a right to demand that
in this most important hour of her life, at the moment when
she presents society with a new member, the labor republic,
the collective, should take upon itself the job of caring for the
future of the new citizen."

-Alexander Kollontai

Several decades of feminist theory have laid before us classic
texts by great writers, every one of them hoping to make a
difference. Yet Germaine Greer (in her 2000 follow-up) noted that
not much has changed in the 30 years since *The Female Eunuch*
(1970) was published. Sexism and its more profound counterpart
in gender remain soldered to every area of contemporary life
both consciously and unconsciously and are not therefore born
or cured by immediate "cause and effect". Their subtlety, indoc-
trination and coercion are too intensive to be remedied by
"enlightenment" and conscious self awareness. These problems
are interwoven with economic and social relations, unconscious
sense and feeling that adjusts the dominant living unit, the
family, accordingly. In the days of larger communal cooperation
workers functioned together as one whole communal entity to
feed and shelter all the other members of the group. This was the
responsibility of all for all. One enormous family unit turned
economically just as the economic unit today consists of one or
two parents sustaining their immediate off-spring. As Engels
demonstrated, alterations in family circumstances perform in
kind to economic arrangements; consequently sexual and gender

relations in the communal families of ancient times were entirely different to today. With the advent of capitalism the single economic unit of labor power shifted from the commune to the individual worker. This singular producer now works under the modern mode of production by which he-and-or she alone are responsible for the family. Socially and to some extent emotionally these conditions are sealed by the regulation monogamous marriage to bear the burden of both labor and familial welfare within this framework.

A more recent example of changes to these relationships is the Russian Revolution. The easing of capitalist relations of production immediately diminished gender pressures and some of their limitations. The fact that there are so many examples of highly successful female artists in the early Soviet avant-garde art is an indication of the diminution of obstacles that appeared to have hindered them, and nearly everybody else, before and since. In contrast to the previous "golden eras" of artistic production such as the Italian Renaissance, sixteenth century Holland and nineteenth century France the early Soviet era dramatically elevated Alexandra Exter, Natalia Goncharova, Liubov Popova, Olga Rozanova, Varvara Stepanova and Nadezhda Udaltsova as a few mentionable major names in the space of five years and whose work has since stood the test of time.

According to Francine de Plessix Gray in her book *Soviet Women* (1989), 92 per cent of women in the Soviet Union were in full time employment and they comprised 51 per cent of the workforce. She says:

"upon the Revolution of 1917, the Bolshevik regime became the first government in history to declare women's emancipation as one of its primary goals, and to inscribe it in its institution. Laws assuring equal pay for equal work...were instantly effected."

Women obtained the vote directly after the 1918 revolution, earlier than the UK. The use of women in manual jobs statistically included "98 per cent of the nation's janitors and street cleaners, 90 per cent of conveyor belt operators, one third of rail road workers, over two thirds of highway construction crews and warehouse workers."

Women also prevailed as over 80 per cent of school teachers and one third of school principals, 77 per cent of doctors, and 50 per cent of hospital administrators and health policy makers, 70 per cent of engineers and technical skilled workers. Good education, high expectations and the respective easing of the glass ceiling in white collar professions ran parallel to the rise of women employed in "working-class" professions. Women were more equal to men in all types of labor.

This question of women and proletarian labor is not frequently referenced but it is important. Wedged between the disparate genres of bourgeois and proletarian work processes lurks the material core of sexism and gender norms as they emerge or are curtailed. These are born in the material fabric and fundamental social formation that is economic, social, political, ideological and, crucially, emotional. One way this is manifest in capitalist law and its merger with paternal law is a prohibition against proletarian labor; a silent legitimacy for its omission. Consequently the question of proletarian labor is rarely mentioned in feminist or even gender theory whose focus tends to be middle-class professions and home-makers. Not broaching the subject lends itself to the tacit agreement that women could and should not perform in many of the more physical working class jobs on account that they are not suitable. The unmentionable negation of this space renders it unquestionable and certified. Female unsuitability and labor takes many forms and number one on this list of unsuitability is the vulnerable nature of the female reproductive facility. The absence of this as a question or an answer renders the resultant theory elite, idealist and vacuous on this particular measure and outside of the real connectivity of the social fabric.

The question of labor leads us to the root of the problem that emerges from conditions under the current system. These conditions are not centered on the producer of labor power, human labor, but on capital. The role of labor, in reality the central core of the production process, is at the behest of economic elements and, as Marx often explained, the worker's physical and spiritual existence is subjugated to the machinery of production. Terence Conran was quoted recently in an interview in *The Guardian* (16 November 2011) that in the 1950s there was "a terrible attitude at schools. They would say, "Johnny, if you don't do your homework you'll end up in a factory" - but what's wrong with a factory?" What *is* wrong with a factory? Nothing fundamentally. It is good work. It is productive. It can or could be interesting. But the capitalist mode of production makes it otherwise. The present conditions for factory workers take their toll on health, for example, and the cost is huge. In France the life span of males in industrial professions averages ten years less than the general population.

How do these facts relate to radical gender studies such as those of Butler (1999). In *Gender Trouble* the question of the economic relationship to gender is dealt with thus; "what political impetus is to be derived from the exasperated "etc"...This is a sign of exhaustion as well as of the ultimate process of signification itself." Meaning class or economics cannot explain gender and that this discourse has its own domain and point of departure.

That gender has its own discrete sphere, rules and determinants is undeniable but they are not fully discrete; they are one of a number of socially composite factors and in this configuration the space of gender abuts that of economics. The point of departure for gender is culturally embedded in social and economic relations as well as having its own formal internal connections. To endow gender with its own sphere of ultimate determination is to re-enter Cartesian transcendence ad-infinitum. To avoid doing this is to ground gender socially and economically in the multiple processes of female labor that comprise the female relationship to the mode of production. Note that in the first instance we steer clear of the dilemma Freud and also Butler have grappled with, that of the problematic of sex and instinct. Emotionally, psychologically or "instinctual" sex and gender can be minimized in their economic relations at least at first and to some extent. The product or use-values related to gender however under the rubric of economics *must* be included in the form of two primary use-values which are child-birth and child nurture.

One would like to embark on a critique of sex and gender distinctions without childbirth but in the economic fabric this forms an overwhelming default power that will always creep its way through the cracks of radical discourse. As such this fabric supports gender, sex and sexing and to deny this does not diminish it. It is the point where the two spheres of capitalist law and paternal law intersect, as the contemporary division of labor fights to assert itself.

Referring to Freud's essay *Mourning and Melancholia,* Butler implies that by the time the natural process of melancholia is initiated the subject is already inscribed within the coercive paternal law. In this schema homosexuality (identification with the lost object in the form of a same-sex parent) is an intrinsically subversive state. Homosexuality is the result of rebellion against the taboo laid down by the paternal law and heterosexuality is the result of the prohibition of this taboo.[13] The homosexual taboo is presumably, according to Butler, already determined even at the point of the very early influence of the narcissistic formation of the ego which in Freud's case study *An Infantile Neurosis* ultimately influences sexuality.

Butler's interpretation of Freud misplaces the mechanism he

explains in psychoanalysis as too conflated with the social. While striving to include a social element herself, the fundaments of the internal relationships between the libido and Ego are overridden in their particular intricacies in favor of cultural determinism. This interpretation is based on a misunderstanding of the social and subversive nature of communication as it functions both consciously and unconsciously. Butler's simplistic schema omits the possibility of political dissension creating subversion against the paternal law on the part of perhaps all sexuality. As Freud expresses in *The Ego and the Id,* the majority of, and perhaps all, individuals are reared in circumstances that instigate bisexuality. This is the result of the to-ing and fro-ing of the lost-object of affection and reclamation as it changes from parent to parent and carer to carer, as demonstrated in A*n Infantile Neurosis* and in *The Ego and the Id* for example:

"For one gets the impression that the simple Oedipus complex is by no means its commonest form, but rather represents a simplification of schematization which to be sure, is often justified for practical purposes, close study usually discloses a more complex Oedipus complex, which is twofold, positive and negative, and is due to the bisexuality originally present in children: that is to say a boy has not merely an ambivalent attitude towards his father and an affectionate object choice towards his mother, but at the same time he also behaves like a girl and displays an affectionate object choice towards his father and a corresponding feeling of hostility towards his mother. It is this complication element introduced by bisexuality that makes it so difficult to obtain a clear view of the facts in connection with the earliest object choice."

Also, in a letter to Fleiss dated 1 August 1899 Freud says:

"Bisexuality: I am sure you are right about it. And I am

accustoming myself to regarding every sexual act as an event between four individuals."

As we can see from this last quote Freud understood bisexuality, though sometimes latent, as a very common phenomenon, thus lending the possibility of a plastic sexuality for many subjects. Butler's criteria of subversion through fundamental forces such as sexing and sexuality should be widened to include the non-essentialist nature of sexuality. This suggests that sexuality and its relationship to gender is also far more relatively linked to social and economic determinants also occurring after childhood via the stimulation and suppression of latent sub-conscious forces. We will argue this is the basis for a critique and subversion that runs counter to capitalism, gender oppression and the paternal law. This subversion is not therefore solely the result of the administration of oppression by the *paternal law* and its particularly anti-female agenda. This oppression and its opposing subversion is based in labor that yields a use-value that has been given the label of "gender", but which in itself has no actual sex or gender. This criteria is what colors the relationship to, and nurturing of, the child and influences the formation of the child's ego. From these circumstances "gender" in its full oppressive political form, is founded on a necessity to bridge the alienated division of labor with the non-alienated, altruistic nurturing and rearing of children. Originating from a distortion of the nurturing use-value, gender enters into ideology, desire, sexuality and feeling as a construct that warps and distorts this initial use-value and eventually the body, sex and sexing. These complexities emerge and are fortified by masquerade and chimera as the inflammation of gender through the displacement and redirection of creative energy in the process of alienation.

A part of this process is the control of the female relationship to nature and to labor which in order to maintain the myth of gender must remain concealed. In this respect females are coerced to be seen to curtail their relationship to matter in the world in the form of their own bodies by the denial of their own sexuality and creativity. This denial is very evident and socially effects the productive input of women in society and culture. It has a bearing on artistic production by creating a limitation to the relationship between the female artist and their materials.

Position of Sex and Gender

Gender is the mediation between the mode of production and sex.

Sexuality and gender can be defined as the following:-

Mode of Production—Gender—Sexuality
Sex and Sexing

That is to say there is a space between the base and the sexual being that is mediated by gender.

To recapitulate some major factors in this relationship. *Society needs to reproduce subjects.* This is a major defining *economic* feature of women. As we stated there is no necessity in the first instance to posit an emotional or even physical essentialism at this point but any theory that purports to include gender must take this simple fact into account. Imperative also is the relationship between working conditions, health and well being.

As Marx says in the 1844 Manuscripts:

"it is clear that the more the worker spends himself, the more powerful becomes the alien world of objects which he creates over and against himself, the poorer he himself - his inner world - becomes, the less belongs to him as his own. It is the same in religion. The more man puts into God, the less he retains in himself. The worker puts his life into the object; but now his life no longer belongs to him but to the object. Hence, the greater this activity, the more the worker lacks objects.

Whatever the product of his labor is, he is not. Therefore, the greater this product, the less is he himself. The alienation of the worker in his production means not only that his labor becomes an object, an external existence, but that it exists outside him, independently, as something alien to him, and that it becomes a power on its own confronting him. It means that the life which he has conferred on the object confronts him as something hostile and alien."

This closely details the disastrous affects of the mode of production on the health of workers as the profit system sacrifices all contingent elements in its own favor. The general physical violence necessary to perpetuate this arises from the base to span all kinds of human activity including reproduction. The labor process is alienating to the body and health of the worker. The detrimental emotional and physical effects on the worker have an impact on the small unit that is the worker's sole responsibility; the family. The family needs the worker's protection both pastorally and financially. Part of this protection is that the alienated nature of the mode of production that the worker labors under cannot be transferred to the family *and most importantly* to the infant who requires protection for their physical and mental development (as Freud demonstrates in his case-study *An Infantile Neurosis*). So an important use-value falls on carers who work within the family unit to protect the emotional and physical health of children from these pressures.

This work is usually performed by women simply because the rules of capital determine that women who take time off work for maternity leave should also perform the nurturing of infants as the principal carer.[14] It is crucial to understand that this is not the result of gender, gender coercion or even child birth but is built on economic regulations determined to maximize profit. Women who need to take time off to have children are of diminishing interest to capital and this factor, in the division of labor, posits them in the role of chief child carer. The potential absenteeism of women in the workplace and the prospect of recruiting and training new workers in turn dints the intrinsic competitive nature of capital. It immediately puts women in a tentative position regarding job prospects without even approaching the question of maternity pay and rights that most companies try and avoid.

Female labor is also construed in a certain light that is emphasized to be of service to this economic situation. According to Marx, labor "mediates the metabolism between man and nature"(*Capital* Volume 1). In proletarian labor natural raw materials are transformed into processed objects of use. Minerals, wood, animals and plants are woven and dyed, mined, refined, smelted, amalgamated, built and eaten. This defines the proletariat as harvesting nature's raw materials by physical labor and transforming it. In their own bodies also, female's biologically generate and combine the raw materials of reproduction to produce human beings. Tallying with the division of labor it is in the interests of capital to draw parallels and emphasize the proletarian aspect of female production. This is that women are akin to the proletariat in that they are the transformers of nature into use-value. This levels women with the proletariat politically, as Engels said, "Within the family, the husband constitutes the bourgeoisie and the wife the proletariat." According to Beauvoir who steers clear of the question of economic coercion in this and therefore is not at all critical, women are more connected with nature than men and with their own animal nature on account of their body and menstrual cycle. This image of women as physical producers who need to indulge their animal instinct by giving birth perpetuates a creature governed by hormones and not rational thought.[15] As Butler says, "reason and mind are associated with masculinity and agency, while the body and nature are considered to be the mute facticity of the feminine, awaiting signification from an opposing masculine subject."

The gain here for capital is that female carers perform the child care tasks allotted to them supposedly as an *instinct* and not an act of labor and therefore should receive no salary. The low-esteem and an imposed concept of the animal nature of this labor means that they require or deserve very little material reward in return for it and are justified as unpaid and unaided in their tasks. As Wittig says, although this service is socially necessary production, it has no exchange value and is therefore "servile labor" and it also serves to justify the receipt of little money from the state for child care or from organizations that employ the husband (Romito 1997).

Note that this situation is in direct opposition to the attitude of the state at the time of revolution. Childbirth, as Kollontai (1921) says, becomes a social responsibility and is classed as a valid form of living labor and not a supplementary or dismissive task:

"Soviet Russia has approached the question of protecting motherhood by keeping in view the solution to the basic problem of the labor republic, the development of the productive forces of the country, the raising and restoration of production. In order to carry out the job in hand it is necessary, in the first place, to tap the tremendous forces engaged in unproductive labor and use all available resources effectively; and, in the second place, to guarantee the labor republic an uninterrupted flow of fresh workers in the future, i.e. to guarantee the normal increase in population.

As soon as one adopts this point of view, the question of the emancipation of women from the burden of maternity solves itself. A labor state establishes a completely new principle: care of the younger generation is not a private family affair, but a social-state concern. Maternity is protected and provided for not only in the interests of the woman herself, but still more in the interests of the tasks before the national economy during the transition to a socialist system: it is necessary to save women from an unproductive expenditure of energy on the family so that this energy can be used efficiently in the interests of the collective; it is necessary to protect their health in order to guarantee the labor republic a flow of healthy workers in the future. In the bourgeois state it is not possible to pose the question of maternity in this way: class contradictions and the lack of unity between the interests of private economies and the national economy hinder this. In a labor republic, on the other hand, where the individual economies are dissolving into the general economy and where classes are disintegrating and disappearing, such a solution to the question of maternity is demanded by life, by necessity."

The Transcendental Feminine

As we discussed, the rules that subjugate the worker to the accumulation of capital often dictate that woman are the main carer of children. On account of economic necessity the wife/mother often performs the use-value of sheltering the infant from the full impact of physical and mental alienation of the dominant mode of production. This is despite the fact that there is no intrinsic relationship between sex and nurturing labor or its use-value. This labor can be equally successfully executed by either sex or gender, however, at this point there is an initial distortion of the nurturing labor in its status as use-value to falsely accord the assignment of the requisite gentle and caring characteristics *specifically* to the female species.

Based on the real platform of the division of labor in capitalism where the female of the family is often, for economic convenience, the main nurturing worker, this labor is falsely assigned characteristics for which we use the term "feminine". This comprises 'caring,' 'soft,' 'sweet,' 'kind' and 'gentle.' This concept assignment at this point in economic relations forms the origins of gender. Part of the necessity to emphasize the characteristics of softness and caring has developed in tandem with the very emphasized alienated characteristics of the mode of production. Thus in recompense to it, the care of the not-alienated, in the form of the care of children, is in direct contrast to it. The pressure is on to emphasize the soft and caring atmosphere to totally protect children not only from capitalist labor and alienation but in an exaggerated form from all labor. Children are the non-laboring perfections who exist outside of labor in capitalism and therefore also need an environment in direct opposition to the alienated atmosphere of the workplace.

The result and combination of these forces is that the nurturing use-value is not only assigned the word and concept 'feminine' but is conflated with it. The closeness at which the two function as words and as psychological concepts such as "feminine" and "caring" for example, often leaves no space for social and economic analysis and is often regarded as natural. The whole feminist movement is an argument over the nature of this space, whether it actually exists or not, of what it consists and complacency or subversion in relation to it. From this origin the conveniences of capital dictate that gender has influence beyond the individual or couple to mold the whole family unit and beyond to conform to it.

To define some essential instances of how this functions we will trace contradictions between the female gender and its origins in nurturing use-value. These are contradictions between alienated forms of labor from the mainstream mode of production and the relatively non-alienated nurture labor. As Marx in the 1844 Manuscripts says:

"The worker becomes all the poorer the more wealth he produces, the more his production increases in power and size. The worker becomes an ever cheaper commodity the more commodities he creates. The devaluation of the world of men is in direct proportion to the increasing value of the world of things. Labor produces not only commodities; it produces itself and the worker as a commodity and this at the same rate at which it produces commodities in general."

This devaluation extends to all forms of labor, even reproduction and nurturing labor. The aspect of labor that unites females with the proletariat as the producer of future workers is particularly devalued. The result is that females are under duress, in order to counter this devaluation and preserve their work status, to perceptually disengage and dissociate themselves from the aspects of their labor that coincides with the transformation of nature by the proletarian worker. Any perceived connection or empathy with proletarian labor therefore diminishes the value of the prime female role of child carer. As a result they must disguise the female relationship to the real matter of production and therefore to nature. Part of this is an emphasis, an overemphasis, on the effete nature of women, their impractical stance and even the prohibition of their material body, energy and desire.[16]

The result of this is that the nurturing laborers must complete their work, while simultaneously disguising any material relationship to this labor. This is the case in the role of women as carers, housekeepers, cleaners and cooks. The real practical duties involving raw foods and chemicals, any physical interaction with them, is sought to be disguised. These are therefore construed socially and ideologically as easy and pleasant tasks that involve no real toil and no real transformation or connection to the mainstream mode or means of production. The disguise of real labor is another factor that aids the lack of payment for such labor. Part of this disguise expands to the physical relationship to nature in the form of the female body itself which is placed in a controlled ideological framework to conceal the reproductive facility. The result of this is the *impractical female*; dependent, unable to perform in practical reality. There is a dominant line in female clothes, particularly *haute couture* that is effete in style and fabric, and shoes are high-heeled and difficult to walk or run in.

As Angela McRobbie (1981) says of high heels, they:

"Make walking, never mind running, a feat in itself; but more than this, symbolically, they represent women's dependent fragile status. They summon up all sorts of ideas about male, chivalry, female bondage; they have an immediate and unanimous resonance of female sexual signs."

Clothing, manners and overall presentation of women emphasize a dissociation from the transformation of raw materials. The fashion and entertainment industries provide policing that emphasizes the pressure of these contradictions to turn them into markets and sell these properties back to consumers. The cosmetics and fashion industries are particularly important in this process. These industries enter the world of culture in the form of dress, manners, movements, clothing, hair styling, labor choice, vehicles, home design, leisure, communication and eventually voice patterns, sounds, facial expressions, smells, and to some extent thoughts, beliefs, sexuality and desire. This prohibition affects the connection of females to the world. The possibilities of their manipulation of materials becomes limited. Curtailed also are displays of energy and passion and these are fundamental to the expression of creativity, particularly within the visual arts. This is further compounded by the 'impractical' nature of women imposed from all forms of culture and fashion. The formation of female gender is supported by orchestrated cultural industries that function to conform creativity, sexuality and gender to the conditions of alienation in the workplace. As Marx says:

"The fact that labor is external to the worker, i.e., it does not belong to his intrinsic nature; that in his work, therefore he does not affirm himself but denies himself, does not feel content but unhappy, does not develop freely his physical and mental energy but mortifies his body and his mind. The worker therefore only feels himself outside his work, and in his work feels outside himself."

As he implies, during the process of alienated labor, mental and physical energy is subdued thus disabling the possibility of the pleasure of holistic physical and mental satisfaction through labor. This embodies a desire to counteract this dissatisfaction in the hours of leisure time:

"External labor, labor in which man alienates himself, is a labor of self-sacrifice, of mortification. Lastly, the external character of labor for the worker appears in the fact that it is not his own, but someone else's, that it does not belong to him, that in it he belongs, not to himself, but to another. Just as in religion the spontaneous activity of the human imagination, of the human brain and the human heart, operates on the individual independently of him - that is, operates as an alien, divine or diabolical activity - so is the worker's activity not his spontaneous activity. It belongs to another; it is the loss of his self.

As a result, therefore, man (the worker) only feels himself freely active in his animal functions; eating, drinking, procreating, or at most in his dwelling and in dressing-up, etceteras and in his human functions he no longer feels himself to be anything but an animal. What is animal becomes human and what is human becomes animal.

Certainly eating, drinking, procreating, etc., are also genuinely human functions. But taken abstractly, separated from the sphere of all other human activity and turned into sole and ultimate ends, they are animal functions."

The physical and mental alienation in the working day results in the desired reclamation of the senses outside of labor. As Marx says, like the working day itself, this reclamation is largely alienated and in direct inverse to the alienation of the labor process. This retrieval of the senses is not made by a renewal of social and emotional interaction, but in the largely alienated forms of mass and popular culture; television, popular music and cinema. Animal and primal functions are manipulated in this sphere through the primal faculty of hypnosis, for example. Hypnosis itself is an important natural phenomenon and a necessary part of evolution. It functions to create the annexation of the individual ego in order to enable the herd instinct to prevail. For this it suspends a sense of individuality in order to sensitize a connection with other individuals in the community. As V. Csányi says:

"In my opinion, hypnotic susceptibility might have evolved as a mechanism for concerting actions of cooperating individuals. It has been a tool to synchronize brain models by non-linguistic means for hominid groups and in that way promote cooperation for a given complex task.

Well-founded hypotheses exist which suggest the appearance of biological communication mechanisms enabling the synchronization and planning of group actions well before the advent of language. An example is mimetics, the enhanced ability of the human face to communicate (Hjortsjö 1969, Ekman 1973), comprising some 250-300 different possible messages and exceeding the communication ability of animals by about a factor of 10. In addition, an extension is the ability of humans to judge intention and emotional state of co-specifics based on the sub-linguistic characteristics of human vocalization like intonation, melody and rhythm of speech (Eibl-Eibesfeldt 1989)."[17]

The alienated mode of production diminishes subtle and harmonious social connection such as are present in environments that develop hypnosis. As we said, the oppression of sense connection and of sensory isolation in the alienated labor process therefore engenders the reclamation of this during leisure time. In modern cultural spaces, properties extracted from the natural process of hypnosis are brutally employed in this. They are distinguished by characteristics of subdued rational faculty with emphasis on repetition; the syncopated beat of popular music, the psychedelic colors of television and kitsch imagery, formulaic "mind numbing" plots, scenes and actors, serve to dull the subject into an alienated hypnotic trance and a brash representation of the natural hypnotic process. These forms of hypnosis lack the subtlety of those made in human group settings. Popular culture often uses sexual desire and arousal for these techniques that result in the redirection of sublimated energy again from the process of alienated labor (Tedman 1999). Freud acknowledged that in the domain of sexuality, hypnotic fantasy is quite easily accomplished. As Rose (1986) says:

"In fact his article (Freud) on the two principles of mental functioning, Freud assigned to fantasy the whole domain of sexuality, whereby it escapes the reality principle altogether..." (referring to Freud's *Formulations on the Two Principles of Mental Functioning*)

The characteristics of this is the kitsch sublimation of alienation by the promise of sexual and gender satisfaction. Satisfaction under these conditions is rarely achieved and crucially therefore the fulfillment of gender is a role that can never be achieved. The expectation of gender as Butler and De Beauvoir put it, of becoming but never actually arriving, reaches ferociously frenzied levels as it is frustrated under the strains of the mode of production and mounts in the face of unrealistic expectation. Any non-conformity to this is thwarted by a menacing dread that stands between gender and the subversion of gender. The result that permeates every industry and facets of family life is that conforming, performing and competing successfully in this alienated state of sexuality (gender) is likely to mean economic success. Failure to comply with this state of alienation and honor gender, in opposition, parallels with failure. Opposition to gender ideology and aesthetics often engenders perceived and real financial difficulty, isolation, low self-esteem, jaded body image, frustrated libido, sexual and professional failure and disenfranchisement. At this point alienation in the form of gender, directly from the alienated mode of production and drenching popular culture, threatens to become a physical, psychic and aesthetic circuit. Subversive sensibility that may counteract it, particularly pertinent in puberty for example, is brutalized as physical amelioration and seduction in the form of needs that satisfy desires take its place.

Within this diaspora however children are protected because the nurturing use-value as a use-value, prevails. Freud's case study is a classic situation of the opposing forces involved. In *An Infantile Neurosis* he says that the father's "affectionate abuse" is at the root of the patient's problems. This abuse, however, is tempered by the early narcissistic ego representation of the "Grusha" memory as a seminal influence in childhood. It contrasts with the "affectionate abuse" of the father, the keynote that strains the patient's infant environment. The dilemma of oppressed homosexuality and its contradiction by early hetero-sexual narcissism together create psychic instability in the subject and encapsulate the dilemma of both protection and exposure to the forces of alienation during childhood. The male and female dichotomy in this particular case study is incidental and the sex of the two chief protagonists in the child's history could equally have been reversed. What remains constant however is the role of the intervention of the alienated mode of production in familial and parental relationships. It stresses the importance of buffering the child from such predicaments and of feelings in the general environment that may be difficult to locate but certainly exist. This takes the form of monitoring and protection from these elements by other carers or self-censorship on the part of the carer so as not to pass on predetermined psychic problems and/or their conjunction and stimulation by stresses in the present. Both of these cases involve alienation either in the immediate or psychic history.

Freud's case histories shed light on how a small lapse in defense against this, of inconsideration or self-indulgence by the nurturer, indicated here as the affectionate abuse of the father, can lead to very long term mental and physical health repercussions in the infant. Therefore every act of consideration on the part of the carer in these circumstances that succeeds in avoiding such forces is political and is a counterattack against the forces of the mode of production. This role of protector and nurturer of the infant against the pressure dealt by the mode of production when adequately completed, is subversive. It strains to defend against alienation and its stronghold that if not rebutted will count costs on physical and psychic welfare. We have noted the roots of this act of subversion and the rebellion against alienation in the mode of production and also therefore against both the capitalist and paternal law.

A miniscule attempt to permeate the endless complexities of this is as follows. As we explained, alienation encompasses the role of buffer and nurturer to create gender and swaddle it in kitsch. The contradictions of this pressure create very complex reactions in the field of sexuality. Elements of subversion against gender-manipulated-sexuality is sometimes aided by latent, pre-latent and post-latent bisexuality or homsexuality.[18] Emotional and sexual plasticity enables empathy for economic and sexual subversion against the paternal law. Latent bisexuality, for example, is often triggered by the constantly oppressive nature of heterosexual pleasure that is merged with economic success and the alienated mode of production. The reaction to ultra-hetero-sexuality creates its opponent and then probably proceeds to remove it again at some point. Nurturers do not escape this and in order to avoid and manage the state of alienation that is being foisted on them quickly understand its contradictions.

Complexities of this kind adjust the gender masquerade itself so that at times it does not straightforwardly tally to the alienated mode of production and can also be a mask, self-refer-entiality, irony, a front and a shield to protect against the inter-action of chauvinism. Just as the laws of physics state that every force has a counter force, so the opposition against the act of labor and of subversion on the part of the nurturer will mount. At some point the forces of opposition take hold and the nurturers themselves must yield to some extent in order to accommodate it and not to be broken by it.

5

Aesthetic World in the Future

"Ideologist, priests, writers are in special spheres in the division of labor and they think they are working in an independent field. And to the extent that they form an independent group within the social divising factor, their output, including their errors exerts in its turn an effect upon the whole development of society, even its economic turn."
Friedrich Engels, letter to Joseph Bloch, 1890.

"In considering transformations a distinction should always be made between the material transformation of the economic conditions of production, which can be determined with the precision of natural science, and the legal, political, religious, aesthetic or philosophic - in short, ideological forms in which men become conscious of the conflict and fight it out."
   Karl Marx and Friedrich Engels, *The German Ideology*.

..."according to the materialist conception of history the ultimately determining factor in history is the production and reproduction of real life. Neither Marx nor I have ever asserted more than this. Hence if somebody twists this into saying that the economic factor is the only determining one, he transforms that proposition into a meaningless absurd phrase."
   Friedrich Engels, letter to Joseph Bloch, 1890.

Any attempt clarify a few co-relations between the mode and means of production and art can be confusing because art is a communicative subject. One needs to be quite strict not to eulogize on this aspect and cross straight over to the role of art as a superstructural and cultural entity and forget the economic relations of production and its relationship to the base. There is a tendency in art history to brush over this too fast and start expressing the affective role of art in culture or of conflating the two, the economic with the cultural, and finally not fully investigating either. Of course it is impossible to talk about both, art and the economic base as totally separate because they are intertwined in reality. A distinction is required however to define the discipline in relation to the base and to comprehend its use-value. At this point its application as a cultural and affective entity becomes pertinent.

Starting With This

The artist works within the dynamic of the mode of production and the economic base. In parallel with all the raw materials used in every kind of production the materials of the artist are also derived from nature. As Marx noted:

> "The worker can create nothing without nature, without the sensuous external world. It is the material on which his labor is realized, in which it is active, from which, and by means of which it produces. But just as nature provides labor with [the] means of life in the sense that labor cannot live without objects on which to operate, on the other hand, it also provides the means of life in the more restricted sense, i.e., the means for the physical subsistence of the worker himself." (*Capital*, Volume 1)

Nature is the raw materials transformed by the artist into objects of use-value. The initial in-put of materials (the materials of the trade), at the point at which they are derived from nature, imparts knowledge and a relationship between the artist and his or her materials. This knowledge, acquired by the artist, incorporates every stage of processing that the materials have passed through, of how to treat them so that the best results are obtained. In these circumstances the artist has optimum control over the materials and how they behave. Optimum control yields optimum results. As with any worker or craft person this sensitive interaction is an important component of artistic production. The experience and immersion with materials with ample time spent to develop it on a full-time professional basis, begins to evolve a connection to them. This experience and interaction affects not only the mind but the body of the artist as it begins to operate on physically sensual, conscious and unconscious levels; the tactile, olfactory, auditory, visual and intellectual are all included. They finally form the actions and approach of the artist as he/she supplants this mediated melangé of sense and rationality and the external material world to a new piece of work.

While involved in the production and transformation of raw materials the artist straddles several classes and divisions of labor. Under the contemporary conditions of artistic production, however, the process of the transformation of art materials from nature has become prohibited to the artist. This process has largely been removed from the artist and is carried out by large industries. This prohibits the artist's relationship to their own means of production, their materials, and therefore hinders the fulfillment of their production of art. Under these prohibitions artists are encouraged to consume, and not produce, what has already been produced and transformed by the industrial base using proletarian labor. This is because under the industrial system, the mode of extraction and transformation of the art materials from nature has already taken place by factory labor before being passed on to artists. The manufacturer has intervened more and more in this transformation since the eighteenth century and has exerted control to conduct and determine it. Part of this control is knowledge. The withholding of technical knowledge from artists. The "secrets" of materials and techniques are held by manufacturers. An example of how this information is curtailed is art magazines. These are reliant on advertising by manufacturers of art materials or they are themselves owned by large manufacturers. This endows the manufacturers with control over these particular modes of dissemination and information regarding the skills and processing of materials. Manufacturers are keen to keep this to themselves and of course encourage artists to buy ready-made products from them, off the shelf. This aspect also merges to some extent with education as it affects and influences the education of the teachers themselves who then pass this on to their own students. There is, therefore, immense economic and ideological pressure to change the artist from being a producer at the fundamental level of production, the level of nature, to a consumer. The work of art that complies with these taboos becomes a work of consumption rather than production and relatively speaking therefore an item of commodity-value rather than use-value.

Despite these changes nothing has changed the artistic necessity and the possibility for a profound relationship between the artist and their materials. The base still straddles the artistic profession via art and the production and connection with materials, its means of production, because despite the pressures of modern industry, the artist's true vocation, remains the trans-formation of these raw materials into objects that function on the sensual aesthetic level. That is, like nature, from which they are derived, they operate at the fundamental level of the senses. As such, the senses themselves are part of nature. This is a return to material truth and origin by the use of materials and as such it has a profound holistic physical impact. So despite the inter-vention of modern industry into art, the use-value of the art work remains the same, it serves to amalgamate the sensual and subtle nature of the perceptive subject at its most profound with the material base, the point at which nature and the materials derive thereof, intercept. The more fully this task is completed, the more work the artist has contributed to acquaint him/herself with materials, the greater the possibility that the use-value of a work of art is realized. Success is based on how well he or she exploits the physical sensual components of the materials and comprehends them sufficiently to reconstruct them to appeal to the sensual body at the point at which both of them originate in nature.

These tasks are performed all at the level of the senses and of feeling as well as ideas because feelings have paramount input into thought, and the production of art concerns both. However, as I have expressed, very scant theory exists that encompasses the role of sensual responses and material affectations of art to the base, nature, the materials derived from it and their construction.

As the human sensual and productive subject is the prime subject-matter in the creation of art, the social role of the artist is to amalgamate the sensual faculties of this subject-matter with the material world. This is enabled through the materials, tools and general working facilities they have at their disposal from the means of production which is part of the mode of production and the material base. The artist is the vessel that supervises these relationships.;

The relationships are approximately:-

External material world Material base Mode of production Means of production	Art-Artist	Human Senses

Divisions of Labor

There are divisions of labor between types of industry and this produces contradictions between them. Art is an industry whose prime purpose is to serve the faculties of perception. This facet forms the main contradiction between the artistic profession and many other industries. When the art industry performs to actually fulfill its job description it is *felt* as a comparison to other industries. Art becomes a practical and real affective indication that other industries, the majority in capitalism, do not seek to serve the human sensual perceptual capacity of the producer. Rather, as Marx says in *Capital,* the human faculties are subordinated to the labor process:

"Man not only effects a change of form in the materials of nature; he also realizes (verwirklicht) his own purpose in those materials. And this is a purpose he is conscious of, it determines the mode of his activity with the rigidity of a law, and he must subordinate his will to it. This subordination is no mere momentary act. Apart from the exertion of the working organs, a purposeful will is required for the entire duration of the work. This means close attention. The less he is attracted by the nature of his work and the way in which it has to be accomplished, and the less, therefore, he enjoys it as the free place of his own physical and mental powers, the closer his attention is forced to be."

Art that is fulfilling its task demonstrates more clearly than almost anything else that the labor producer in the mainstream industrial system subordinates him/herself, his sensual and intellectual potential, his "own physical and mental powers" to the labor process. By its very profound contrasts and differences art thus demonstrates on the level of feeling that subordination in capitalism involves servility to the division of labor. Also, from 'Estranged Labor' in the *1844 Manuscripts*:

"The worker becomes all the poorer the more wealth he produces, the more his production increases in power and size. The worker becomes an ever cheaper commodity the more commodities he creates. The devaluation of the world of men is in direct proportion to the increasing value of the world of things. Labor produces not only commodities; it produces itself and the worker as a commodity - and this at the same rate at which it produces commodities in general."

The very existence of this art is also proof of the existence of a sensual environment made primarily for the sensual and mental values of the human faculty and the possibility of this. Art that provokes this sense therefore also provokes a series of strong and disruptive feelings in relation to the production process. This disruptive effect ripples out to become a general deviation to the ideological and aesthetic/culture-base quagmire that drives the worker to continue in his role, as Marx says, "as a machine". This is the truly revolutionary component of art. It contradicts and in some way threatens to destabilize the "normality" of capitalism. A disruption to the "reproduction of the means of production," a sort of revolution for the senses.

In this kind of antagonistic environment the capitalist understandably becomes alarmed. The first and most self-beneficial instinct of the capitalist is to keep art tightly under lock and key in private collections in order to control and pacify this material and its threat to the dominant mode of production. These conditions often take effect from within the art industry itself which is often funded by other industries. The production of art is also controlled and sometimes antagonized from within its own sector by its own state and business components. There is a tendency to champion artists who do not contradict the dominant mode of production. To support and encourage artists who do not fully utilize their medium to stimulate the perception of the body of the producer of sensual labor power. These are artists who, although professional and highly deft with materials, base their work in language, symbolism, conceptual cultural puns, popular culture, and cross-referencing and tend not to incorporate the relationship between humans and nature and therefore the economic base and the subject. Their work is based in dominant ideology. So although they are often critical and skillful within their particular medium they do not use these skills to investigate and stimulate the sensual relationship between the conscious and unconscious subject and nature. They begin in the alienated discipline of ideology and popular culture and the linguistic narratives derived therein. On the level of the senses therefore these artists often pander to and even valorize alienation in this capacity. (This is heavily influenced by a largely Lacanian outlook that the subject is already always alienated as soon as they are formed socially.) Formally, their art work also panders to the mode of production and therefore does not contradict the separation and alienation between artists and their materials made by manufacturers.

The selective political component in the art industry takes control via posts in teaching institutions, funding, exhibitions and publicity. Artists who do not tally to these measures are subject to lack of appointments to teaching positions, curatorial censorship and rejections for grant applications. Artists who fall outside of it are not encouraged financially or otherwise to proceed and as a result of being without economic sufficiency are more likely to be deterred from the profession.

Likewise the profession of an artist in the *more profound sense* is a non-profession in capitalism. This is because artists that contradict the dominant mode of production and fulfill their job description as artists are undermining the way their own class makes its bread.

These factors combine with the result that art that is really doing its job, fulfills its job description and actually appeals to the senses is quite rare in our society. The level of discouragement and evasion in the present means that the producers of quality are often unable to continue.

The majority of artists are unable to pursue the immense artistic task of negotiating the sensual subject with the mode of production. They go the easier route by moving the goal posts. They move the sensual subject *nearer* to the mode of production.

As a result these artists do not have such a large space to negotiate between the mode of production and the sensual subject, and their job is far easier. In this way these artists officially diminish the sensitive and profound nature of the senses of the human subject and reinvent them newly formatted to suit their task and also to suit the tasks of alienated labor. They invent a personality for whom the height of artistic appreciation comes from a more shallow and brutal species than actual human sensuality. This type responds best to jokes, pastiche, parody and narratives referenced in popular culture. Artists usually end up bringing their work down to the ever encroaching and bullying and mainstream dominant mode of production. The most important and original dumbing down.

So the negotiating equation has the artist situated in this instance not equally between the subject and the mode of production but much nearer to the mode of production and they drag the sensual subject or a convenient representation of the sensual subject along with them.

The production of art that fulfills its task is the opposite of this. It drags the mode of production nearer to the sensual subject so that the mode and means of production, the materials, methods of construction and ideas, all *serve* the sensual subject. This dragging, when it does happen, involves a tampering with the dominant mode and means of production within art practice. As we have discussed in Chapter 2, the work of Yves Klein is an example of this. He and his chemist colleague Edouard Adam worked to understand and manipulate the materials of color production at a fundamental level and then to present them in formats that serve the senses, that is, that have the pressures of the mainstream mode of production removed. This is a contradiction to the base. These artists challenge capitalism with a contradiction to the base unlike artists who, from the point of view of materials at the sensual level, pander to it.

Modern Artists

As we stated, the majority of contemporary artists who are supported by state, industry, publicity, education and the gallery system do not particularly tackle the contradictions in art such as they relate to the dominant mode of production. They work painlessly and in comparative harmony within the criteria that is acceptable and available within this system. They evade the issue of the relationship between materials and the sensual body to a small but crucial extent to concentrate on the narrative, story, concept, shock, concept, or surrealism. These works often merge easily and quickly into mainstream advertising and cinema. As we said these artists move the human senses nearer to the mode of production, by dumbing the senses down within their art works and not the other way round which is the revolutionary artist who seeks to stand firm with regard to human sensuality and move the mode and means of production nearer to it. To move the mode and means of production nearer to the senses, however, is too much for many artists, too heavy a weight to bear and they avoid awareness of its existence even psychologically, they block it out. These artists do not stand in defiance of the prime objective of the dominant labor process in capitalism partly because to do this involves the difficulty of being treated as a non-artist, a non-worker and a non-existent person. As Marx says:

"Political Economy regards the proletarian ... like a horse, he must receive enough to enable him to work. It does not consider him, during the time when he is not working, as a human being. It leaves this to criminal law, doctors, religion, statistical tables, politics, and the beadle. ... What is the meaning, in the development of mankind, of this reduction of the greater part of mankind to abstract labor? What mistakes are made by the piecemeal reformers, who either want to raise wages and thereby improve the situation of the working class, or - like Proudhon - see equality of wages as the goal of social revolution?"

Equal violence subjected via the division of labor to the proletariat is also visited on artists who place themselves on the side of the proletariat as part of their contradiction with the contemporary economic base. Under these conditions artists evolve into a second profession who, alongside the proletariat, are also extracting and transforming materials from nature to endow it with use-value. The result is the continual striving and necessity for the capitalist to try to erode the rights of both these groups and hence also erode the value of their respective labor power. Part of this process is to disguise the respective value of each of them. In the art world this disguise is apparent by the almost total omission of the labor and material aspect of production of art in the realms of art theory, art history and the presentation and policing of the work in art galleries.

As we expressed, many artists in contemporary society find themselves unable to negotiate the huge space between the sensual subject and the means and mode of production. They often solve this with a shift in their conceptual and practical propagation of sensual life within their art practice. Art which seeks to stimulate the interconnecting human facility of perception and color perception is not often realized. *If the antagonism of the space between the mode of production and human sensuality were lessened, however, the affects of the difficulty of negotiating the space would immediately begin to cease also.* For example, if profit was not the central concern of dominant industry. If the capitalist's voracious appetite for labor no longer existed. If the producer of labor-power was the owner of his own labor and if labor were acknowledged and not denied its rightful position as the central force in the transformation of raw materials from nature. If these were the case the whole art industry would therefore no longer stand so strange and so isolated from the mainstream mode of production because its core values of appealing to the sensual system would no longer be so different to other industries. With sensual labor power acknowledged as the central force in the transition of raw materials from nature, the whole labor process would be geared toward tailoring the working process to herald the worker and his and her labor-power, and not as it is at the moment, making the worker subjugate his and her self to it.

With the space between art and the dominant relations of production lessened there would therefore be less pressure on the artist whose work it is to mediate the two spheres, the mode of production with the sensual subject, and many contingent effects and forces that prohibit this would also be lifted in kind. There would be less suspicion regarding art, less protection and policing of it, less elitism. There would be a diminishing of artists and art performing in a brutal capacity that conflates human sensuality towards the mainstream mode of production. Instead of creating this thug-like view of human sensuality, many more artists would stand firm regarding the value of human sensuality.

Art of long term appeal and consequence with its rare sensual qualities would no longer be so rare in this environment, immediately de-constructing the artist as genius, and the transcendental nature of aesthetics in its relationship to the material world of production would be clearer and less abrasive to visualize. As well as this, the whole concept of art would change so that it would be almost unrecognizable by today's standards. This would be because of the fundamental changes in the production process and its rippling effect onto the whole social network.

Firstly, changes in the mode of production would create a different relationship to artists' materials yielding a greater choice of materials. This is because art materials and the basic processes of their manufacture would not be so stringently limited by the means of production.

To explain the full significance of this it is necessary to briefly acknowledge once more the extent that art stimulates the senses through the use of materials and color relations (in a way described more fully in Chapter 2); that the multitude of color in the environment has evolved human perception to discern countless colors, shades and textures. These perceptive capacities commandeer the whole body because in evolutionary terms the body, senses and mind evolved via a succinct scrutiny of the natural world and the vast multitude of colors and of substances which are its formal vehicle. The production of art involves an intensification of these facilities. The artist chooses pigments and substances to appeal to the capacities of the body to enable it to be stimulated by its natural properties in an intensified fashion.

The natural world and evolution with its vast number of substances and colors contrasts with the limitation in mainstream capitalist production where a very narrow use of a number of pigments and colors are reused time and time again. These are omnipresent in the designed and built environment. They are usually produced as a by-product of the oil industry, by vast multinational companies who currently hold monopolies and thus have vast control over the color-making process. The relatively few colors they produce are based on the most profitable for the manufacturer, as the cheapest, most lightfast and quickest to fabricate. They form the basis of the majority of colors in paints, fabrics, furnishings, clothes, printed material, shop fronts and interior design. This limitation and presence creates a jarring and sensually brutalizing atmosphere in the human-made environment by its limitations on sensual perception. Thus it contradicts and dulls sensuality as it has evolved by interaction with the millions of colors and textures such as are provided by the natural environment.

With the forces of capital, competition and profit motives lessened, the production process would no longer be held by such limitations. The lifting of economic and industrial restrictions that currently thwarts and limits the production of pigment production would immediately widen the number of pigments and colors available particularly for use in the designed and built environment. An expanded number of available textures and colors would begin (relative to the present day) to rival the numerous, countless substances and colors in the natural environment upon which evolution and the thriving of the human nervous system is based.

The result would be that the designed and built environment would also benefit from an increase of colors and textures. This would affect fashion fabrics, vehicles, architecture and interior design as the whole designed and built environment would not be so far away from the subtlety of color and materials in nature, and also therefore not so distant from the work of art as it now stands.

The artist who spends a great deal of time working on and discovering a wide range of materials and their effects would now also be, relatively, more likened to the profession of industrial color producers. The production of pigments in industry would not be such a separate process (again relatively speaking) from the artist. The techniques of pigment production that belong to a section of the division of labor, often controlled by industrial manufacturers at present, would no longer be limited and artists therefore would have more access to it. The extraction of materials from nature would no longer be classed as 'proletarian' labor in terms of its vast distinction from that of the present day 'artist'. Manufacturers, now less bent on profit, would no longer keep their processes of production secret for fear that the artists acquire them to begin making their own materials and thus erode profits. Education itself would be raised in this area. Restriction in reading matter, particularly industry-controlled art magazines, would be lifted. A sensual relationship between the artist and the materials and techniques of industrial production would allow artists access to the gamut of tried-and-tested methods and materials of the masters of antiquity and also modern methods of production.

An example of how these possibilities could come into play is observable in some recently completed art works. Among them, as we noted earlier, is the work of the artist Yves Klein who, as we also explained in Chapter 2, used the industrial process of color production in his own art practice and therefore removed it from the immediate manufacturers' necessity for profit. The environment in general therefore could be much nearer to this very type of artistic labor. This would mean the effects of what we now call a work of art, with its succinct and sensitive nature, would not be so unusual and not be regarded as so incredible, ethereal, transcendental or godly to become more generally dispersed and available in society and throughout society, in all walks of life from the factory shop floor and the coal mine to the high street. Architecture, design, decoration, and building materials would all have fine or high art or a move toward artistry running through them. Shop fronts, clothing, painted surfaces, fashion, ceramics, interior design, architecture, paints, car design and all forms of culture would change to edge slightly nearer (always on a sliding scale in relation to the economic factors) to art, a little closer to an Yves Klein type quality of painting with its independence of the current restrictions of production.

Art itself as an entity will no longer be floating in space, with its abstract and "useless" qualities. The whole world transformed into minor works of art, these would become more high grade as the situation progressed. As we said, the works of art in galleries would lose their rarity and 'priceless' qualities to the extent that now exists. The concept of the transcendental genius artist would quickly fade, mainly because the attack on this at the level of feelings induced through art, design and the environment are very profound ones. This would likely deal a fundamental death blow to all forms of bigotry closely connected with concepts of innate greatness and its reinforcement of divisions in the class struggle.

Possibilities in Architecture: Jean Prouvé

The drawing together of the mode of production with the demands of the sensual subject would not only change artistic production but all disciplines connected with art and design. Architecture, for example, would edge nearer to art in the same way that works of art by Yves Klein embrace the world of industrial production. The French architect Jean Prouvé demonstrated examples of these possibilities in architecture, parallel to those pursued by Yves Klein.

Born in France at the turn of the century, Prouvé was one of a number of highly influential artists, architects, interior and furniture designers who came from or congregated in France in the first half of the twentieth century. This list also includes Charlotte Perriand, Delaunay-Terk, Le Corbusier, Picasso, Pierre Jeanneret, Amédée Ozenfant, Oscar Niemeyer, Fernand Léger, Alvar Aalto and Berthold Lubetkin. In France young apprentices are encouraged to learn a chosen skill while maintaining their cultural and intellectual development and it was clear from the beginning in Prouvé's case that he would acquire expertise in several disciplines. He was later keen to shape his public image around the idea that he was not married to a specific aesthetic or discipline. The tenets of *l'École de Nancy*, the arts and crafts association founded by his father and godfather were a powerful influence, "I was raised," he said, "in a world of artists and scholars, a world which nourished my mind."

Prouvé was apprenticed to a blacksmith and then as a metal-worker at Szabo Metal Works and in 1923 opened his own studio in Nancy to produce wrought iron lamps, chandeliers and hand rails. Prouvé's advanced expert technical knowledge led to the installation of the town's first ever arc welding machine that began to develop his keen interest in aluminum materials and marked the start of his move into furniture design. He began using prefabricated and interchangeable modular pieces to make the furniture, such as the metal desks designed for the *Compagnie Parisienne d'Électricité* in 1926, techniques that were to distinguish his later architectural work.

In 1930 Prouvé was involved in establishing the *Union des Artistes Modernes* (UAM) a group of French modernists who had become disillusioned with the conservative and salubrious concepts of the older and more established *Société des Artistes Décorateurs* (SAD).[19] They embraced modern production methods and Prouvé soon adapted another state-of-the-art electric folding machine specifically for the purposes of his own production. The first of the *Ateliers Jean Prouvé* opened in 1931 with immediate success and he began collaborating with the architects Eugène Beaudoin, Albert Laprade, Tony Garnier, Robert Mallet-Stevens, Le Corbusier and Marcel Lods on projects such as the *Maison du Peuple* at Clichy. During the Second World War while active in the resistance, Prouvé continued to develop technical innovations manufacturing bicycles and the *Pyrobal* stove that burns on any fuel. It was this continued success throughout the war that enabled him to begin applying the newly discovered electric welding methods to *architectural techniques*.[20]

The Housing

In 1944 Prouvé opened a factory at Maxéville devoted to specialized aluminum research and experimental housing. Prefabricated housing was not itself new, it had been around since the Tudor era and was widely used in post-war Britain. Prouvé's particular technical knowledge, however, combined with his aesthetic sophistication, made his vision of this type of housing unique. He began to manufacture modular housing units, using combinations of materials as an aesthetic and technical extension of his furniture designs. These units thus benefited from the influence of his most illustrious collaborators such as Charlotte Perriand and Sonia Delaunay-Terk. The aluminum and steel designs of the American designer Raymond Loewy were also a major influence and he was encouraged to import this aesthetic into housing using the streamline curves of cars, ships, rockets and planes.

One major technical advance stemmed from Prouvé's furniture designs made from sheet metal and other metallic parts. He originally used these to decorate buildings designed by avant-garde artist associates. A key engineering innovation in these designs was the successful manufacture of sheet steel of extreme thinness, less than one millimeter thick. Two sheets of this formed a "hollow body" of great strength and resistance such as used in the reclining chair of 1929. A further innovation, explained by his assistant Bernard Collet, was the corrugated roof design of the *Maison Tropicale,* specifically made for the warm tropical climate. The channeled shape of the roof enables air conditioning to circulate in these houses without the need for any electric system and thus remain naturally cool in the hot weather it was designed for.

Prouvé's own family home was built by the architect himself and still stands on a grassy hillside overlooking the city of Nancy in North-East France. For economic reasons the house was constructed from assorted fragments of modular housing panels that were the residue of larger projects undertaken at the factory at Maxéville. These panels mainly comprised of wood, reinforced glass and the trademark Prouvé metal panels with circular windows. This diverse combination of materials and texture are formally united under the modular format of standardized panel size, each of them precisely one meter wide. (This was a constant panel width throughout all Prouvé housing.) The contrast lends a sculptural and yet systematic quality to Prouvé's house at Nancy reminiscent of the three dimensional designs by artists of the Russian avant-garde or modernist sculptures by Mary Martin for example.

Formal sophistication is not at the expense of technical expertise, however; it entirely merges with it. The aluminum panels and their multiple in-built round windows, for example, are non-corroding, relatively light-weight and are sandwiched around an interior wooden structure filled with insulation. The originality of the unique circular fragmented vista gained through these windows also serves distinct technical needs simply because a circular cut-out is easier to precisely adjust than a right angle cut-out. The large rectangular windows are made from reinforced glass that insulates the house effectively against the Northern French winters.

There are many advantages of pre-fabricated housing. The low cost of production is due to the fact that they do not require cemented foundations, such as is the case in brick-built houses. Consequently there is no need for structural engineers, nor prohibitions against certain soils, such as clay for example. The buildings are erected very quickly, within days, or less, without specialized labor skills. They avoid the problem of traditional brick housing and its low tensile strength that does not bend and twist easily and is therefore prone to problematic cracks, particularly unsuitable for earthquake zones and extreme weather conditions.[21]

The Failure

In 1945 *Ateliers Jean Prouvé* was commissioned by the French Reconstruction Ministry to mass-produce frame houses for refugees. These pre-fabricated industrial buildings were made from aluminum and shipped to Africa where 800 were erected, each of them by three non-specialists within four hours. Another type of house, the *Maison Tropicale,* was also designed for use in Africa but was never fully commissioned and only three were eventually built. Despite the cost-effectiveness, efficiency and desirable nature of the housing, Prouvé's architectural project was not a major success. As the *nancy.urbanism.chez-alice.fr* site explains:

1 "His work did not stop at the simple logic of profit, and tended towards the accomplishment of social and cultural ideas, which was more akin to a form of "enlightened craftsmanship". And that while he also wanted to "make a house like a car". This met with fierce resistance from governments, regulatory bodies, building technologists and architects."

The French government had decided that prefabricated housing should be not be put into mass production as a remedy to the severe post-war housing shortage. They instead showed preference for tower blocks as a means for housing the population. Prouvé ran into financial difficulties and called in the company that supplied him with aluminum sheets for fiscal support. His control was marginalized, however, and shortly afterwards in 1954 the doors of the factory were closed on him for the last time.

Prouvé's enterprise was destined to failure precisely because of its attempt to merge the sensual subject with mainstream market forces. The bridging of these two poles require too much effort to be maintained for any length of time. In Prouvé's particular project difficulties manifest through several routes:-

1. The long history and tradition of bricks and mortar housing has evolved many auxiliary industries to support them. These range from the production and processing of raw materials, such as cement and brick mining and manufacture and extends to the building of the houses themselves. This forms the backbone of many established construction enterprises who are extremely hostile to any competitive concepts that may encroach on them.

2. Prouvé's type of inexpensive, easily erected, desirable and potentially bankable housing could potentially solve the housing shortage and thus in turn cause property prices to drop. Again, the fiscal security of many of the most established enterprises including banks are based this. Expensive and selective ownership form the mainstay of these industries and any disruption is a threat to a considerable political and financial power base.

3. Prouvé's ran his factory under different methods, for example, after the reinvestment of any profit into the development of the business, the total remaining sum was shared among the workers.

4. The division of labor in capitalism extends to education and to transgress this is itself a contradiction. Prouvé achieved this partly because he was born into it through

the art movement his father directed and because of the general education system in France. As stated, school leavers are highly encouraged, obliged in fact, to learn a practical trade if they do not want to continue in academic education. This, however, does not preclude them from returning to academic courses after a year or so of training. A philosophical as well as an artisan aspect is incorporated into these trades in France as they merge slightly more towards academic disciplines. Divisions between practical and theoretical work, at least at the level of training, are slightly less strict than in the United Kingdom for example. As a result it is more evident the means by which this architect was able to acquire comprehensive knowledge of technical engineering, art, design, architecture, interior, furniture and industrial design, as well as art and design theory. As we explained above, this combination was paramount in the designer's work output and he was able to utilize and tailor the production process to evolve useful and aesthetic designs that were workable and efficient at the level of production and in practical use.

Conclusions

Prouvé's work provides an example of the possibilities for architecture and the accommodation of an aesthetic that connects directly to the industrial process. The work of contemporary artists and designers was merged here with a concept of mass produced architecture by Prouvé. These were then altered to accommodate the mode of production in an attempt to create a *human centered sensual environment* also with the potential to be *replicated at an industrial level* and thereby thoroughly disseminated and used outside of elitist and selective artistic environments. Its use was meant to extend beyond the walls of art galleries and restrictive income groups and professions.

The revolutionary nature of this project in its time did not tally with the contemporary mainstream mode of production and consequently the enterprise was abandoned. It is an example of the breaking down of divisions between education and also types of production. The mode and means of production was created here to serve the senses and not to serve (relatively speaking for what was still a capitalist enterprise) profit, competition and conformity to vested interests. The difficulty of making it a success can be explained as the present division and gulf between these two realms, the sensual subject (the producer of labor power) and the forces necessary in successful capitalism. In other words it is the manifestation of alienation in the production process, in architecture and the environment.

This breaking down of the industrial process to serve the sensual subject in the realms of architecture parallels the work of Yves Klein in artistic production. However, when the two industries of art and architecture are no longer so antagonistic to each other then general design in the environment will veer more towards fine art just as fine art will gradually be more integrated through design and industry. It calls to mind the medieval pre-capitalist era when the quality of artist and artisans work was high. The role of artist did not exist as a separate profession as it does in modern times but merged with artisans' work in the ancient basilicas and churches for example. Just as production in this era was hand-crafted and slow, however, the modern industrialized version would be fast and potentially egalitarian in availability and counts as a truly "enlightened craftsmanship".

Despite its immediate commercial failure Prouvé's project is referred in architecture schools the world over to demonstrate the aesthetic possibilities of industrially manufactured housing. The very rarity of this in twentieth century Europe is an indication of the stranglehold on aesthetic processes from competitive enterprise. Prouvé's project demonstrates the potential in the production process of closing this space by egalitarian methods that eventually approach high works of art.

J.M.W. Turner as Producer

With human perception at its kernel, the art industry is unusual. Unusual in comparison to industries that have speed of production, cost effectiveness, the accumulation of surplus labor and profit as the prime assets that enable their success. Success in these industries is largely based on how efficiently they comply with the forces of competition in the pursuit of capital. These forces permeate the art industry too, and make an undeniable mark on it, but the art industry has different criteria for success: the appeal to the sensual subject. Real success in the art industry is when art fulfills its criteria to appeal to the sensual subject and this success has far less direct or essential relationships to the mainstream forces of production. Success in the art industry is therefore largely dependent on its counter-force against the forces of the capitalist mode of production. This chapter contests that art works made by J.M.W. Turner are examples of this success and this counter-force. This is because Turner upheld his professional assignment to produce items with the key tenet of appealing to the sensual subject despite the pervasive influences of the forces of production. I will explain why a prime source of this accomplishment is the substances and techniques that Turner used to construct the art works. The materials define his own and the viewer's relationship to the painting via the means of production and therefore the transformation of the raw materials of nature into a potent and affective force for both parties, a use-value. In this transformation the art industry operates on the same level as all other industries that involve the productive transformation of the real materials from nature to use-value.

This investigation into the particular use-value of art is made possible by combining two associated concepts of Karl Marx. In order to explore the artist in his/her contemporary productive environment we follow the relationships drawn by Marx between philosophy, ideology and the economic base expressed for example in *The German Ideology*. As Marx says:

> "We set out from real, active men, and on the basis of their real life-process we demonstrate the development of the ideological reflexes and echoes of this life-process. The phantoms formed in the human brain are also, necessarily, sublimates of their material life process, which is empirically verifiable and bound to the material premises. Morality, religion, metaphysics, all the rest of ideology and their corresponding forms of consciousness, thus no longer retain the semblance of independence. They have no history, no development; but men, developing their material production and their material intercourse, alter, along with this their real existence, their thinking and the products of their thinking."

Marx's notion of "ideological reflexes" is combined with his concept of alienation as developed in the *1844 Manuscripts* which, as discussed earlier, then effectively gives birth to a new additional level to those sited by Marx; an aesthetic level of practice (Tedman 1999). This level probes economics, philosophy and ideology and, crucially, the transmission and exchange of these between perceptive and reactive subjects. This exchange is fundamentally trafficked between these levels by the materials that construct the subject; the body. It entails the relationship between the body and the senses and how these are influenced. The aesthetic level thus analyses affectations on sense and feeling from each of the levels, as experienced from the inside, from the sensual body, which is the physical and material instrument of the perception of these levels and their unifying feature. Demonstrating the heightening or subduing of this corporeal mechanism enables the development of Marx's concept of alienation to be based in the physical and psychic body and not in the spirit, as it is often interpreted.

I will explain in detail how the artistic means of production, the materials and techniques used by Turner, have an affect on the sensual subject and on perception. This will clarify how the artist as a producer on the aesthetic level of practice connects in a material relationship to the base via a sensual reaction to physical matter, the materials and techniques, thus emphasizing a reaction to substance rather than ideas. Of course an understanding of the artist's out-put on all of the levels; economic, ideological and philosophical is required for a history of art but this text wishes to incorporate, though not overemphasize, that which is normally omitted: the input of sense and feeling in this process.

It must be said that this text concentrates on defined aspects of material sensuality and the role of art materials in these. It is therefore necessary to narrow down the analysis of Turner's work to a specific study of his materials and techniques and to display this area in depth. As a result, in this particular study, the paintings of Turner are the main concern and the importance of his watercolors, drawings and lithographs are largely passed over in their favor. As it is necessary to analyze the material construction of Turner's output as it reaches an abstract and formal state the focus is narrowed again to a very few paintings when the characteristics and techniques discussed appear most relevant.

Another feature of this text is that it concentrates on the formal materials and technique and, though it is necessary to understand these in the context of narrative and figurative aspects, the latter is not emphasized in order to focus on the former.

The Order Of The Text

To express the foundations for these relationships we initially explore the conditions of the economic base that Turner worked in during an explosion of industrialization in Britain. We adhere to Marx's premise in *The German Ideology* and how, as he says, these conditions affected the realms of thought and ideas. In the philosophies of the time these are mainly idealist and utilitarian concepts used to furnish the expansion of power of the bourgeoisie and manufacturing industries. The relationship of the base to philosophy is then traced through to the realms of contemporary art history with the theories of Winckelmann, Bellori, Craske, Alexander Gerald and Edward Young.

The result of all these forces are seen in Turner's practice inside the Royal Academy of Art which sought to control his education, technical production and specifically the methods he manipulated and the material substances he used.

The Economic and Philosophic Conditions

The immense increase in productivity and industry that ran parallel to the life of Turner was summed up by Marx in *The Poverty of Philosophy*:

"In English society the working day thus acquired in seventy years a surplus of 2,700 per cent productivity; that is, in 1840 it produced 2,700 times as much as in 1770. According to M. Proudhon, the following question should be raised: why was not the English worker of 1840 twenty-seven times as rich as the one of 1770? In raising such a question one should naturally be supposing that the English could have produced this wealth without the historical conditions in which it was produced, such as: private accumulation of capital, modern division of labor, automatic workshops, anarchical competition, the wage system, in short, everything that is based upon class antagonism."

As Marx says, the era is characterized by enormous advances in industry, invention, science, medicine, manufacturing and population growth and also by enormous exploitation of workers and the denigration of their working conditions. These conditions in Britain in particular enabled the Industrial Revolution to flourish. Britain became the world's leading power, controlling one quarter of the world's population and one fifth of the total land area and London became the most populated city in the world.

As Marx and Engels say, the phantoms that inhabit the mind are found in the real lives of men so therefore it is possible to trace the origin of Descartes to the contemporary conditions of the base. His philosophy provides the epistemology for the entrepreneur's position in the division of labor. Descartes suggests that the attainment of truth and also God is entirely cerebral, and not through sensory signals, that:

"bodies themselves are not properly perceived by the senses nor the faculty of imagination, but by the intellect alone"...and the..."soul is absolutely distinct through our notions of the body" and "the mind by which I am what I am is wholly distinct from the body."

With regard to this Descartes further posits that the world cannot be:

"properly perceived by the senses nor the faculty of imagination, but by the intellect alone."...and..."whether awake or asleep, we ought never to allow ourselves to be persuaded of the truth of anything unless on evidence of our reason, and it must be noted that I say of our reason, and not of our imagination or our senses."

This was the first modern strike in the battle of abstract capital over labor within the discipline of philosophy which Kant later reinforced in *The Critique of Pure Reason* (1789):

"And just in this transcendental or supersensible sphere, where experience affords us neither instruction nor guidance, lie the investigations of reason, which, on account of their importance, we consider far preferable to, and as having a far more elevated aim than, all that the understanding can achieve within the sphere of sensuous phenomena."

In *The German Ideology*, Marx and Engels define the relationship between economics, the real material conditions and philosophy by Kant's economic and class interests:

"We find again in Kant the characteristic form which French liberalism, based on real class interests, assumed in Germany. Neither he, nor the German burghers, whose whitewashing spokesman he was, noticed that the theoretical ideas of the bourgeoisie had as their basic material interests a will that was conditioned and determined by the material relations of production. Kant, therefore, separated this theoretical expression from the interests which it expressed; he made the materially motivated determinations of the will of the French bourgeois into pure self-determinations and moral postulates."

The British empirical philosophers Locke, Hume, Bentham and Hobbes were also the product of the advanced growth of manufacturing in Britain. *The German Ideology* notes that:

"The advances made by the theory of utility and exploitation, its various phases, are closely connected with the various periods of development of the bourgeoisie."

As Marx observes, the strongest influences for these philosophers are utility, efficiency and practicality and also transcendental relationships to God, perfection and the innate sensual
inability to truly perceive the material and sensual.[22]

Marx contradicts these philosophers in terms that merge
reason with the sensual. He says that there is a holistic subject at
the center of these conceptions and that in the process of alienation the human source of labor-power is made estranged from
his/her own sensual self. These concepts were explored prior to
Capital in *1844 Manuscripts* where the term "alienation" describes
the estrangement of the subject from him/herself. This
estrangement has sometimes since been labeled as 'pre-Marxist
humanist Marx'. Tedman, however, has designated the thesis of
alienation as sensual and physical estrangement brought on
through the estranged labor process. This alienation from the
sensual body thus frees it from the criticism of transcendent,
spiritual alienation and humanism.[23]

Further Investigations into the Philosophical Level: Art History

If as Marx says ideas are the product of real material conditions,
how did they manifest in the branch of philosophy known as art
history? Winckelmann states in The *History of Ancient Art* (1995):

> "The highest beauty is in God; and our ideas of human beauty
> advances towards perfection in proportion as it can be
> imagined in conformity and harmony with that highest
> existence which, in our conception of unity and indivisibility
> we distinguish from matter."
>
> And beauty is the "loftiest conception of humanity..."

This strong influence of transcendental philosophy is also
clarified in the work of the art historian Giovanni Bellori (1615-
96) who followed the notion of God as the "high and eternal

intellect". This considered the transcendent perfection that artists must attempt to achieve as "noble painters and sculptors imitate that first creator, and form in their minds also an example of superior beauty and reflecting on it, improve upon nature", where nature is composed of imperfect forms and that the artist will "take from diverse bodies all that which in each single one is not perfect. Since it is difficult to find a single one which is perfect."

Writers of the period continued to emphasize the artist as the possessor of an exceptional mind able to connect to "superior beauty". According to Craske (1997) notions of originality and original genius were promoted from 1760s onward, with, for example, Alexander Gerald's *An Essay On Genius* (1774) and Edward Young's *Conjectures On Original Composition* (1759). Parallel with philosophy, art history also emphasizes the superiority of the mental processes in a founding role for real beauty, truth and God and hence to produce art. This is how the "real economic conditions" create thoughts and ideas in the realms of art history. The capitalist's quest and necessity to conceptually overwhelm labor-power with abstract ideas meant that the emphasis on idealist notions of transcendence are devoid of relationship to the real material conditions of production. An artist formed through his education, peer pressure, political and historical influence and his general place in the relations of production are all ignored and overridden by "genius". The artist is an individual genius not only devoid of the imperfect sensual world but also hindered and thwarted by it.

The Effect On The Production Of Art

The growth of industry during the Industrial Revolution meant that the production of paints and grounds were increasingly being made by mechanical methods and were no longer hand-made as they had been in the guild system. The success of companies such as Winsor & Newton and Daler-Rowney furnished the financial power to fund several newly formed art societies. These societies promoted mechanically, ready-made art materials among artists by potent means that became a forceful presence in the art industry. For example there were competitions and awards from the Society of Arts for the development of machines and processes that hastened production.[24]

Craske notes that *The Society for the Encouragement of Arts, Manufacture and Commerce* funded prizes, schemes and public exhibitions where artists began to rely on the award of contracts and commissions from the public and private sector and that "seeking a competitive edge caused the modernists to encompass many innovations in commerce". Furthermore, state-of-the-art development of tubes of paint arrived in 1841 and "was taken up immediately by city colormen who soon enlarged and invested in new "manufactories" with the latest steam powdered grinders and impact extrusion machinery."

As Barrett (2008) argues:

"In an age of unbridled capitalism, society found artistic commercialism acceptable and painters thus employed the newest methods and materials, greatly assisted by a new generation of suppliers and technicians..." "After the invention of tubes industrialization began in earnest and economies of scale soon began to apply, providing much better quality, stability and practical standardization of the product..." "By the 1850s artists' paint manufacturing was big business, as seen by the rise of many major international trading firms in London, Paris and Düsseldorf and the huge success of Winsor and Newton meant they could reinvest in the newest machinery."

This effected art education. The guilds diminished and with them the thorough education they had offered young artists. The long apprenticeships needed to learn about preparation of materials were no longer available. The in-depth craft skills of pigment grinding and understanding the characteristics of various types of oils and resins and the vast possibilities of a variety of grounds and varnishes were increasingly lost. Craft knowledge and skill was now chiefly the reserve of colormen who were becoming ever more industrial. In the interests of technical superiority manufacturers guarded their knowledge regarding materials and techniques. Profits were based on manufactured products so they had little interest in promoting the traditional skills that flourished for many centuries before colormen existed. As Harley (1970) says, in the early seventeenth century the workshop tradition was still strong allowing painters to acquire knowledge of materials; however, by the eighteenth century they had little information to add to their training and when eventually literature was produced it was often unsatisfactory. Complaints began to arise from artists, regarding the state of their own ignorance and on the low quality of some manufactured art-material products.

As Townsend (1999) points out:

"This transition coincided with both a social and conceptual change in pedagogy, wherein art instruction shifted from the private to the public domain, and away from the practical to the theoretical."[25]

Artists from then on had less social and professional contact with the artisan trades because, as Harley says:

"the social status of painters had changed and artists were no longer classed as artisans, they dissociated themselves from much that was practical or mechanical..."

As artisan skills succumbed to mechanization and the artisan trades separated away from the fine art trade a notion began to overtake Europe that painting and sculpture were elite skills by comparison to the other artisan professions. This resulted in the professional and social separation of the fine artist from other artisan trades and the popular notion of the artist as a genius isolated from his social and productive context flourished.

As the old art guilds diminished, academies of art were set up in their place. As Barratt explains in his excellent study:

"Academies were originally organized by states to regulate the training and development of artists. In the broadest sense, they wrestled the production of art away from a guild controlled, church-sanctioned mechanism to an academic system sponsored by the state."[26]

The struggles and contradictions between the economic, ideological and philosophical conditions in the artistic mode of production were by now acted out in the most important English academy, the Royal Academy of Arts,[27] the oldest art school in England. The institution was founded on a Royal Decree by George III. Except for the premises, originally given by the King, it received and still receives no state support. Its income is derived from exhibitions, endowment funds and by sponsorship from commercial and industrial companies and also finance from subscriptions of friends and corporate members.

This struggle in the Academy was especially potent because, despite pressures on artists and the prizes, grants and patronage from manufacturers providing encouragement to artists to use manufactured art materials, some members and associates, such as George Field and Charles Eastlake, actively advocated the education of artists in art materials and techniques. They rigorously bemoaned the failing quality of some manufactured materials and sought to educate young artists in traditional methods of preparation.

Turner

How were the economic, ideological and philosophical levels mediated by individual production on an artistic and aesthetic level? As we shall see this aesthetic mediation of the mode of production with culture is made through the means of production, which is: the artist and their art materials. Here our means of production takes the form of a specific artist, Turner[28] who was a sensual subject operating on this level, and his resultant choice of art materials.

Turner first exhibited a watercolor at the Royal Academy in 1790, when he was fifteen, and soon after he was elected an Associate. As an artist born about 100 years after the break up of the guilds and also therefore without a formal system of training, Turner's education regarding art progressed under his own volition and with the patronage of customers in his father's shop[29]. From his youth, Turner worked with his friend and contemporary Thomas Girtin on the technique of watercolor. Turner and Girtin are said by the biographer Thornbury to have advanced the use of the medium to the extent of being the real founders of the art of water-color. In 1795 the pair abandoned the technique of the monochrome base with local color laid on over the top and the order of application was reversed so that local color tints were laid first and shadows after. Paintings by Girtin showed this change in 1802 and also Turner's *Edinburgh* in 1804.

Turner next turned his attention to oil paints and according to the Turner specialist at the Tate Gallery, Joyce Townsend, he had a very limited range of colors as a young painter which was probably the result of isolation as a craftsman and lack of knowledge of the best sources of materials. Following other young contemporary artists he learnt by gleaning information from manuals, from fellow artists and perhaps from his neighbors in Covent Garden; the local colormen and theatrical scenery designers. Despite this lack of formal education, throughout his life, Turner became known for an unusually thorough interest in art materials. In 1800, when he was twenty-five, Turner employed an Italian colorman named Sebastian Grandi to train him. Grandi had been directly trained in the techniques of the Venetian masters of the old guild system. Among his teachings he showed Turner an antiquated and complicated process to produce an "absorbing ground" for painting.[30]

Turner also filled many notebooks with information on the chemistry of pigments, paint and ground recipes. According to Townsend, this indicates that quite early on he was not using colormen to make his materials and was attempting innovations by making them himself. He relied heavily on advice from Field and Eastlake for this. By observing artists such as Titian he noted that grounds pervade through the paint and produce a particular affect, according to their color and texture. I have seen a number of notes on grounds in Turner's sketch/note-book inventory at the Clore Gallery Library, including details of a ground used by Rembrandt in his painting *Good Samaritan* which has, as Turner says, a "brown (asphaltum) ground that pervades through the sky."

As we expressed, Turner began his oil painting career, like other artists of the period, with very little technical knowledge regarding grounds, pigments and stretchers. His early works such as, *Holy Family 1803* and *Venus and Adonis 1803-5* consist of techniques that are not very different from those of other painters of the period such as Barry and Haydon. In contrast to Turner's later works the layer underneath the paint of his early works, the ground, is thin and just sufficient to cover and protect the canvas. Holmes traced the technical development of this when:

"we find that Turner's youthful works are elaborately executed with much glazing. In the middle period the ground becomes lighter and the pigment thinner,... As time goes on the loading of the ground becomes heavier and heavier, while the superimposed colors become thinner and thinner, till his method at last becomes a transparent one."

This did not evolve with ease according to Holmes, for example, Turner's earlier advances with white oil ground caused his paintings to darken until eventually, after years, he was able to develop a thick white oil ground that retained luminosity. As his career progressed however and Turner followed his interest in materials he experimented extensively with the effects of many media, wax and resins and as a result new techniques began to emerge. By the time he painted *Northam Castle, Sunrise* around 1845 this was very pronounced. The ground is now white, thick and rough. The paint consists of many thin layers one on top of the other. The unfinished *Venetian* scenes of 1839-45 also, for example, consist of overlapping thin areas of white paint, using a variety of media and tone, pure white, pearly white, pale yellow, pale gray.

I have made up an oil ground following the same ingredients and method as Turner, which contained flake white pigment, linseed oil, glue size and water. It is a difficult ground to make and needs to be mixed in a particular order so as not end up with an unusable 'scrambled egg' type mixture. The flake white pigment and gesso must be mixed together first, with the glue size dissolved in water and added afterwards. Even when made correctly this ground is a viscose, lumpy, jelly and needs to be applied and pressed into the canvas with a spatula rather than brush. The ground is very luminous, it remains very white on drying and provides an uneven but resilient surface.

Turner's interest in the "phenomena of vision and of how the sensual body perceives and performs, becomes apparent through his use of materials which were combined with his advanced empirical knowledge of contemporary physics and physiology.[31] This manifests in Turner's ground and paint techniques and can be observed in art works which evolved through his specific interest in the physics of perception as expounded by Newton's *Opticks*. In 1665 Newton contended that the variety of light and dark colors displayed on the surface of bubbles was due to the thickness and closeness of their inner and outer surfaces. This was confirmed later in experiments by a contemporary of Turner, Thomas Young. He passed a beam of light through two separate pinholes and then reunited them. This resulted in dark and light tones, as the peaks and troughs in the wavelengths either reinforced or negated each other. The diversity of the colors and shades on the surface of bubbles were therefore shown to be dependent on the variety of these wavelengths colliding. Thus emphasizing the integral nature of color perception and matter (the thickness of the surface determines wavelength and therefore color) in the phenomenon known as interference, in which Turner had great specific interest.[32] To this end, as Townsend has explained, Turner's technique is an attempt to build up paintings optically, that is to say, using numerous layers with various opacity and pigment loading. An example of this is the unconventional use of bitumen in the dark shadows of *The Opening of the Walhalla*, exhibited in 1843, coupled with an almost pure wax medium and water. Oil and wax were often combined with a number of gelled media to yield different levels of transparency for glazing and for the 'contrasting refractive index of the resin components ' (Townsend). To emphasize this Turner would also utilize a combination of application methods in one work, including his own thumbnail in *Walhalla* for example, and knife painting, thick impasto, scumbling and thin glazes such as used in *Rain, Steam and Speed* of 1844 to create a variety of surfaces.

The pictorial representation of interference in the atmosphere of some of his works, therefore, is made by these materials, wax, resin, megilp and by the variety of application methods.

Yet Turner's works are not only pictorial representations of interference phenomena. The eye of the viewer really does observe interference in the form of the contrasting media that manipulates the light. Placing different medium together creates different levels of real interference with each medium having a new affect on the wavelength, on the color and on the eye, and Turner's particular luminous, reflective and rough ground aids in this process. The profound subtlety of color changes through the various media in these works, and is manipulated by the skill Turner acquired through many years of learning experiences with materials and their effects. The very slight changes in color according to media built up layer after layer enables the viewer to perceive the various factors of change very delicately, sometimes in ways that are imperceptible rationally but are still there as a sense, affecting the body and the unconscious.

Conclusions

The radical reaction against this aspect of his work is well documented. Firstly, that this fastidiousness regarding materials was unusual at the time is clear from comments made by fellow artists and observers. Turner and his father, who prepared Turner's canvases to his strict specification, were ridiculed as parsimonious and "mean" for producing their own materials and became the butt of jokes at the Academy. One account says Constable was "afraid" to ask Turner what bizarre substance he was using on his canvas. "The sea looks like soap and chalk" was a newspaper comment on the painting *Calais Pier*. Other references to his paintings included *The Snow Storm* exhibited in 1842, described as "soapsuds and whitewash" and other works as "cream or chocolate, or yolk of eggs, or currant jelly," "eggs and spinach" and "mustard," and his later works in particular were often casually referred to as "mad" which as Hardy suggests probably caused him much distress. Opie said in 1804 of Turner's *Boats Carrying Out Anchors and Cables to Dutch Men of War*, that the water "looked like a turnpike road over the sea". Jokes that renamed Turner's work were common in the press as Thornbury explains:

> "Mr. Thackery had laughed in "Ainsworths Magazine", at *The Napoleon and Rock Limpet*. Mr. Gilbert à Beckett, who laughed at everything sacred or profane, laughed at Turner's *Udine and Masaniello* in his *Almanac of the Month*. He calls it a "lobster salad", and says Mr. Turner mixes his colors on the canvas or pelts it with eggs. He calls it a "fair specimen of the slap-dash school". The drawing represents him painting with a mop and bucket."

According to G. Reynolds (1969) it was precisely Turner's inventiveness with method and his handling of oil paint, that accounts for the difficulty his contemporaries had in understanding him.

By 1831 most of Turner's uncommissioned exhibits were coming back unsold from the Academy on account of the extreme style of the work. One visitor to Turner's gallery published the "terrifying" details of the "bizarre" abstract works causing him, the viewer, to flee the premises. So Turner's relatively non-figurative pieces, that concentrate on painting technique while minimizing the pictorial element, generally received a bad reputation in his day.[33] This reception was in vast contrast to his contemporary, the painter of melodramatic and cataclysmic scenes, John Martin, who was referred to by Lawrence as the most popular artist of the time and by some admirers as one of the greatest geniuses that ever lived. When Turner exhibited his more "abstract" works they were sometimes booed by the public and often criticized by the press, which was documented by Thornbury:

> "I append some of the cleverest of these attacks on the dying lion [Turner], to show how clever and how cruel they were: "Trundler R.A. treats us with some magnificent pieces.

(1862);""No.77 is called Whalers by J.M.W. Turner, R.A., and embodies one of those singular effects which are only in this artist's pictures. Whether he calls his picture Whalers, or Venice, or Morning, or Noon, or Night, it is all the same thing as another. (1846)"

After Turner's death these abstract works were judged *not* to be paintings at all and were stored in a separate room. This continued for about one hundred years until the paintings began to be recognized.

I suggest this situation bears witness to the force of the presence of the industrial mode of production, ideology and philosophy within the artistic domain and in the Academy. Originating from the economic base, this is the sum of the artistic manifestation of alienated labor through the superstructural entities of philosophy ideology and art criticism. Economic forces emerged from the powerful art retail industry on whom the Royal Academy of Art was particularly dependent. These forces were reinforced by the philosophies of the period that fundamentally sighted the "natural" nature of the split between the mind and body, and between thought and the physical. In this schema, thought, the mind and reason had a more profound relationship to truth than that of feeling and the senses. In the case of art history in particular, truth was deemed only to occur through the intellect and dreams of the artist and had nothing to do with material practice and construction.

These forces combined within the art profession to result in the split between the artist and their materials. The physical skilled labor of production was placed on one side of the transcendental divide, and the "refined", conceptual and intellectual notions of "high art" on the other. The break was now regarded as "normal" with Turner ideologically and emotionally "abnormal" for opposing it. Turner's motivated practice enters the realms of aesthetics and feeling I suggest, because some of his works profoundly combine the bodily separatism brought about by the driving force behind this situation: the division of labor.[34] This is accomplished via the profound sensual effect of the color and materials in the use of media of various opacity and their stimulation of the eye and conjoined physical responses. Turner himself rejected these divisions in his practice and theory to "step outside of his own field" and familiarize himself with the contemporary science of perception as well as in depth research into materials.[35] The true artistry in the work of Turner is his ability to profoundly combine this knowledge at the aesthetic level in his works of art. We reiterate that to a relevant extent Turner rejected the dominant economic forces that removed materials and techniques from artists and therefore also rejected and negated the ensuing effects of this in ideology, philosophy and art theory. Forces that were dominant in the Royal Academy with its dependency on corporate funding at a time when art material manufacturers were thriving and powerful. Turner therefore averted the base-dominated ideology and aesthetics by pursuing the *appropriation of art materials and knowledge of techniques back from the manufacturers.* In transgressing the division of labor in his practice and in his production, by understanding materials to the extent of countering physical alienation in his work, the ensuing art works also transgress the manifestation of this division of labor as alienation on the artistic level.

Turner therefore fulfilled his professional assignment by completing the task of making objects whose core intent is directed towards human sensuality. These transactions took place in the art industry where the artistic use-value posits human perception at its nucleus. It is at this point that the means of production within the art industry becomes potent as a real affective force. The art materials define a sensual relationship with the painting, for the artist and the viewer. It verifies the artistic mode and means of production in relation to the various autonomous levels; economic, philosophical, ideological. Turner has an affect on these in a profoundly critical manner through the material sensuality derived from his production.

Turner stood guard and successfully rebutted within his practice the aggressive economic commercial pressures of the base at the level of perceptive and bodily feeling. The majority of the resultant radical reaction against his work was not because of his subject matter, his narrative and figurative content, but because of *the way* he painted it.

The consequences of this have also permeated theory via the domain of art history. Until the present day Turner is often understood as weird and vulgar with regard to his physical and sensual interaction with materials, or on the other hand, as a great lofty genius. I have found little attempt to join the 'two' sides of his 'practical approach' and 'mind' together and his pursuit of materials as outside of the 'normal' is not counteracted in these writings. Turner's progress through the unity of materials, techniques and observation remains obscure. Michel Serres notes that Turner as an artist was interested in matter and wanted to paint the "reality of fire," and also that "painting and matter triumph over geometry and form". Serres fails to distinguish between the *pictorial representation of fire* and real fire and also omits the role of art materials as part of Turner's artistic interest in the *substance* that makes the representation. This leaves the unchallenged notion that Turner, in an ethereal capacity, was somehow able to capture fire or light while his technical engagement is ignored. This is echoed in the book *JMW Turner: A Wonderful Range of Mind* when the writer says Turner "had been particularly successful in seeming to mingle light itself with colors." There are also many attempts to promote Turner in the idealist schema as having a "great mind". *The Oxford English Dictionary of Art* says he was a "most original genius" though with minimum reference to the relevance of construction. This is not remedied by the majority of the few existing books and passages about Turner's technique that reiterate that he was penny pinching and mean with regard to materials. A contradiction to which, however, is found in Joyce Townsend's exceptional study of Turner's methods at the Tate Gallery that states that he often bought wildly expensive lapis lazuli ultramarine pigment as opposed to cheaper substitutes.

This details how economics produces (and is reproduced by) a sensuality that underpins ideology, *not* as a set of theoretical instructions given didactically to subjects but as elements that manipulate the sensual, the bodily and feelings. In the same way that Turner and his contemporaries such as Haydon and Fuseli make their position within these circumstances known or felt through what they produce and also how they produce, all other cultural producers to some extent do the same. The effect of this ultimately influences subjects, and, as Tedman (1999) points out, becomes part of their affective practices, present in their movements, voice intonations, glances, manners and expressions, modes of dress, and also in the textures, factures, shapes and colors they respond to, in the works of art they admire, and, *if* they are artists *in the art works they produce.*

It is through these influences that many artists throughout their lives have felt the dominance of the Cartesian-based aesthetic and ideology of separation between mind and body, both outside and inside the academy, in the development of the division of labor, and the ensuing philosophy and art theories integrated with it, as the "correct" way, the way things truly "are". The influence of this is then borne out in the artists' methods and works, where they have felt that the maintenance of the separation of the artist from the materials and the occlusion of the potential physical effectuality of this in the art work, to be "normal". Part of these feelings take place at an unconscious level as part of their formation and like every other subject Turner and his contemporaries had had a lifetime of experience of this honed by the education system in the aesthetic state apparatus (ASA) on their road to becoming artists and finally having it influence their work.

It is particularly important to have this process recognized, especially in an art institution, because of the nature of the work of art and of artists, whose occupation it is to manufacture pure or intense keynotes in culture, in this case within the ASA of the Academy. It enables a more accurate understanding of Turner's situation within this framework, of the political act of his particular antagonistic key-note toward many in the Academy, the dominating forces portrayed by his colleagues in their "affective practices". Armed with this we can now go back to the beginning of this chapter with an additional and more intrinsic sense of the intertextuality of the various factors and forces within the art world and also within the wider scope of the reproduction of ideology and of economic conditions.

Turner imprinted his own ideology and aesthetic onto external objects by the choices, approaches and techniques in constructing the work. This imprint therefore has an affect and effect on the sensual feelings of the person who encounters it. These feelings are then disseminated to other subjects so that they either reinforce or deter, but certainly stimulate, the feelings of others, everyday choices and eventually politics. Battles take place when opposing forces of this kind come into contact with each other and clash.[36] [37]

Our analysis of the role of this particular aesthetic state apparatus, the Royal Academy, is made possible through a review of the artist's technique. It indicates the trafficking between base and superstructure on the level of primary vital force, the human nervous system, as an aesthetic. This is strategically necessary to acknowledge within an art institution because of the nature of the work of art and of artists whose occupation is to manufacture pure or intense keynotes in culture, in this case within the aesthetic state apparatus of the Academy.[38] [39] The separation of artists from materials in the industrial system is an economic condition of the division of labor that remains difficult for the artist to counteract, but it is the aesthetic fortification of this that makes it still more arduous.[40]

Notes

1. The distinction between different disciplines need to be remembered while using this methodology. As Marx says in *Preface to A Contribution to the Critique of Political Economy:*

    "In considering such transformations a distinction should always be made between the material transformation of the economic conditions of production, which can be determined with the precision of natural science, and the legal, political, religious, aesthetic or philosophic - in short, ideological forms in which men become conscious of the conflict and fight it out."

2. A biographical comparison of De Hooch and Vermeer seems to bear this out. Despite his fame as a Delft genre painter, De Hooch only remained in Delft for a short period, before eventually settling in Amsterdam which had a large bourgeois population and a flourishing art market. Here he changed from genre painting to scenes of lustrous buildings. He also continually sought commissions from members of the art-buying bourgeoisie and was successful in this: one Delft linen merchant, for example, bought eleven of his works. By comparison, Vermeer always remained a resident of Delft and developed his painting technique with no abrupt changes in style of subject matter. He appears to have actively avoided attempting to earn a living from his work and only painted at most about two or three works a year. Most of these remained unsold at his death; however, even if they had all sold, they would have yielded only about a quarter of Vermeer's necessary income. He is instead likely to have lived by art dealing and the assistance of his mother-in-law.

3. Vermeer was not the only practitioner with this approach in Holland at the time. His fellow Dutch contemporary

Spinoza writes: "Most writers on the emotions and on human conduct seem to be treating rather of matters outside nature than of natural phenomena following nature's general laws. They appear to conceived man to be situated in nature as a kingdom within a kingdom."

I suggest these sentiments coincide with Vermeer's as he presents the natural phenomena of color interaction and perception at the expense of the ideological interests of the moment.

It is interesting that even among the very few facts known about Vermeer, there is some evidence that he and Spinoza moved in similar circles. Both, for example, were acquainted with Christian Juygens, the founder of modern optics, and Karel Fabritius, Vermeer's teacher was taught by Rembrandt, who was himself a friend of one of Spinoza's tutors, a liberal rabbi called Manasseh ben Israel.

4. For a similar discussion under different semantic labels see Jean Piaget's book *Structuralism*. This is a consummate account of the relationship between a variety of disciplines. Piaget explains and draws the many threads of "structuralism" together from their disparate corners. He explains how the godfather of structuralism De Saussure spawned a particular strain were the langue or associative elements, the "deep structure" was sometimes attributed to the arbitrary "surface structure". This aspect was then taken in isolation from the rest of Saussure's work and applied in quite a vulgar manner. Levi-Strauss for example does in the realms of a social subject like anthropology without sufficient clarification as to an integral relationship between the deep and surface structures. I also had a deep discomfort with "structuralism" applied in this way. The formal terms ascribed rigidity "pasted over the top" of things that do not suit it and this is brash and without subtlety. Structuralism should be depicted from connections observed from the inside. This

is the Spinozin and Engelsian philosophy of our organic relationship with nature. Where we came from and how it shapes our minds and bodies. This is about uncovering the rules that exist but not about inventing and imposing them. In other words they impose and conflate deep structure on to the arbitrary to become a kind of vulgar formalism.

5. According to the *Oxford Dictionary of Art*: "Poussin also made it his endeavor to achieve a rational unity of mood in each picture and developed a theory of modes akin to the current theory of musical 'modes' supposed to be derived from antiquity. According to this theory the subject of the picture and the emotional situations depicted dictate the appropriate treatment which can be worked out rationally and consistently according to the principles of language."

6. The metaphysical nature of thought and related mechanisms such as language are what perhaps makes this distinction made by Saussure necessary. Although, granted, there is the possibility of examining the path of electro-impulses of thought within the brain, the actual content of each impulse is not conceivable until part of a larger whole, it is impossible to designate a particular impulse to a particular thought outcome. The complex path of brain impulses and their relationship to the content as physical is not conceivable. Although it is a product of physical matter, thought, conceptually, almost falls into the category of the metaphysical, until it is expressed the thought can only be perceived as flesh and electricity, but still it is a thought. This points out the difficulty in applying time to actual cognition, because conceptualization itself is impossible to find except in its relationship to other things, and is perhaps why people like Saussure, dealing with a cognitive subject, concentrate, not on the temporal but on evidence of the synchronic, static pattern available. The synchronic is therefore a non-linear, topographical measurement. This is

perhaps also the reason why other types of analysis of perception often take the synchronic form, for example, psychoanalysis itself is outside of time when Freud pinpoints key moments from the history of the subject. Here the examination of the non-linear relationship of the psyche and its transgression of the temporal or diachronic in the form of memory is retained and recalled to and from the subconscious. The transactions for these processes are also described in the non-temporal topographical illustration of the *Ego, the Id and the Superego* where Freud says the subconscious has no concept of time.

7.   "We see the co-ordinations formed outside discourse differ strikingly from those formed inside discourse. Those formed outside discourse are not supported by linearity. Their seat is in the brain; they are a part of the inner storehouses that makes up the language of each speaker. They are associative relations." (Saussure, p.123)

8.   The notion of syntax is knowledge centered on the brain, the head. To understand syntax as a mental capacity not a feeling capacity is reinforcing the Cartesian. However, culture is steeped in the transcendent its influence reaches into science, humanities of all disciplines and it is difficult to think or write beyond it. As Chomsky says: "it may be that contemporary natural science already provides principles adequate for the understanding of mind. Or perhaps principles now unknown enter into the functioning of the human or animal minds, in which case the notion of a physical body must be extended, as has often happened in the past, to incorporate entities and principles of hitherto unrecognized character. Then much of the so-called mind-body problem will be solved in something like the way in which the problem of the motion of the heavenly bodies was solved, by invoking principles that seemed incomprehensible or even abhorrent to the scientific imagination of an

earlier generation."*Rules and Representations* p.6.

Syntax is an instance that is felt as physical and not just "in the head" but dominant Cartesian epistemology has hindered understanding of this. As a result of this syntax is sometimes taken in transcendent terms as mathematical abstractions in the brain. This is only the case however if one sees the brain and the body as separate. If the mind and body are not separate but work in unity then syntax can be described as somatic also.

9.   "Let us picture a living organism in its most simplified possible form as an undifferentiated vesicle of a substance that is susceptible to stimulation. Then the surface turned towards the external world will from its very stimulation be differentiated and will serve as an organ for receiving stimuli."..."It would be easy to suppose, then, that as a result of the ceaseless impact of external stimuli on the surface of the vesicle, its substance to a certain depth may have become permanently modified, so that excitatory processes run a different course in it from what they run in the deeper layers. A crust would thus be formed which would at last have been so thoroughly 'baked through' by stimulation." Sigmund Freud (*Beyond the Pleasure Principle* p.297).

10.   More on the opponent process: The opponent process states that there are three pairs of unique sensory reactions - red-green, yellow-blue and black-white; no member of the red-green or blue-yellow combination can be active in the same receptor at the same time as its complement. Hering's explanation for the negative afterimage was that when, for example, a red stimulus to the eye is withdrawn, the red process stops and automatically starts the opposing process, creating a green sensation.

11.   The armor has also been systematically balanced and spaced from black to white in equal measure, from white

gray, gray white, gray black and black gray across the surface of the painting.

12. Generally, when popular culture is employed there is no utilization of the senses in the fashion of Uccello's painting where the effect of the color and factural relationships incorporate the whole body and its connections. Interrelationships which are stimulated homogeneously and holistically. A process that subtly encompasses the all facets of the body so that they are not alienated from each other. The effect of this is in contradiction to popular culture which fulfills an equal and opposite force to the mode of production. It creates a cultural normality at the level of the senses, on the aesthetic level which is an agent for normalizing the alienated mode of production. The profuse nature of this aspect of popular culture creates a sort of sensual prison for the body both ideologically and aesthetically. It is a sensory anesthetic (Tedman 1999) that sublimates the feelings of the pain of physical alienation derived from the labor process.

13. Contrary to the way this is set out in *Gender Trouble* Freud does not mention the taboos in the texts cited by Butler such as *Mourning and Melancholia* or in other related ones such as *The Ego and the Id*.

14. Science itself is sometimes known to comply in this task with researched evaluation into the kind and caring "female" hormone oxytocin as opposed to the aggressive male substance "testosterone". The biological roles are on one level, they are not unconnected from mental attributes like creativity for both sexes.

15. De Beauvoir sees birth and women as animal act; page 89 of *The Second Sex* states, "For it is not in giving life but in risking life that man is raised above the animal;" she then explains that man brought home the fish, made canoes out of tree trunks, man did all the hunting according to her,

however this has now been found not to be quite true. As we point out in pre-history there were no families as we know them now. It is possible therefore that child care was not the role of the mother or even the grandmother or even particularly of women. Recent discoveries have proved that women were hunters in primitive societies.

There is now evidence that women were not particularly the child carers and we can visualize that prehistory was a world free of our particular ideological slants (with ideological slants of their own).Women of 28,000 years ago for example are acknowledged to have been the technologists and also perhaps the artists of society. For example the Venus figurines, art objects from 28,000 years ago, suggest that women may have been the authors of the famous stone age figurines. These figurines were recently found to have weaving on them and it is established that women were the weavers of those days and nets were also woven by women enabling them and also children and older people to catch small animals such as rabbit and other game. Women are the most likely authors of these figurines because of the detail of the weaving on the images and in order to depict it one would need to have knowledge of weaving. (*New Scientist* - Roger Lewin 06/05/2000; Adovasia and David Hyland at Mercyhurst College. Olga Soff - University of Illinois at Urbana-Champaign)

Also in:

Farewell Man The Hunter - *New Scientist* Volume 177, issue 2376 4.1.04 Originally from *Journal of Human Evolution* (Volume 43, p831): "Some of the latest information suggests that men were probably not hunters, they were scavengers and women mothers and grandmothers were probably involved too. Many bones bear the cut marks of human utensils and also animal tooth marks suggesting the animal was killed by another animal first before humans drove off that animal to eat it. Also it is suggested that mothers and grandmothers needed to look for food also (particularly in drier areas where meat was scarce). The biological roles are on one level, they are not unconnected from mental attributes like creativity for both sexes."

16. *Origin of The Family Private Property and the State* 119-120: "In public law the state also does not recognize the family, up to this day the family only exists for private law. And yet all our histories have hitherto started from the absurd assumption, which since the 18th century in particular has become inviolable, that the monogamous single family, which is hardly older than civilization, is the core around which society and the state have gradually crystallized."

17. More from Csány V. (2000) on hypnosis: "The basis of the second group of the new characters, which exist also only in man, is quite a few mechanisms serving the synchronization of the activity of group members. Such is the ability to imitate. That property of man that he is willing to copy behavior patterns observed without any reward or a goal which very seldom occurs in its pure form in the animal kingdom. In most of the cases imitation is not conscious. Usually, copying is not exact, but concerns some parts of a complex behavior form or just taking a few characteristic elements from it. Imitation exists in all human cultures.

    Susceptibility to hypnosis also belongs to this group, enabling control of one another by means of a close emotional bond and, according to recent findings, this is not a unidirectional communicational channel but a bilateral one..."

18. The fuller version of the quote from Freud on page 372 of *The Ego and the Id: III The Ego and the Super-Ego*: "For one get the impression that the simple Oedipus complex is by no means the commonest form, but rather represents a simplification or schematization which, to be sure, is often enough

justified for practical purposes. Close study usually discloses the more complete Oedipus complex, which is twofold, positive and negative, and is due to the bisexuality originally present in children: that is to say a boy has not merely an ambivalent attitude towards his father and an affectionate object-choice towards his mother, but at the same time he also behaves like a girl and displays an affectionate feminine attitude towards his father and an affectionate object choice towards his mother, but at the same time he also behaves like a girl and displays an affectionate feminine attitude to his father and a corresponding jealousy and hostility to his mother."... "In my opinion it is advisable in gender, and quite especially where neurotics are concerned, to assume the existence of the complete Oedipus complex. Analytic experience then shows that in a number of cases one or the other constituent disappears, except for barely distinguishable traces; so that the result is a series with the normal Oedipus complex at one end and the inverted negative form with one or other of its two components preponderating. At the dissolution of the Oedipus complex the four trends of which it consists will group themselves in such a way as to produce a father-identification and a mother identification."

19. Despite considerable debate about the relationship between art and industry the *Société's* long-standing commitment to the luxury end of the market resulted in considerable tensions between its more conservative members and others more sympathetic to modern design principles. This led to the establishment in 1929 of the ideologically opposed *Union Des Artistes Modernes*, that was committed to design production and consumption that firmly embraced new materials, manufacturing technologies, and the realities of modern life. Acknowledging the significance of modern design, in 1930 SAD invited the *Deutscher Werkbund*(DWB)

to exhibit in Paris. Amongst the DWB designers on show were Walter Gropius, Marcel Breuer, Herbert Bayer, and László Moholy-Nagy. Although the SAD continued after the Second World War its position never regained the vitality and sense of purpose of its earlier years.

20. Prouvé's approach to design and making was systematic. Both the design process and the look of his design were of equal interest to him. He produced flow charts for the factory at Maxéville. These showed exactly how materials and elements moved from one machine to another and how one procedure followed another, from the stocking of sheet metal, rubber and neoprene sections, right up to the product's dispatch. Tools and materials were categorized by the making process: cutting, punching, bending, plating, stamping and welding. Also his frame-by-frame photographic documentation of each experimental building project allowed him to refine the product and its construction. Later in life he founded *Constructions Jean Prouvé* whose major works included a café in Evian, a pavilion for the centennial of aluminum and the Abbey Pierre house. In 1953, Prouvé designed the facade of the restaurant of the Hotel de France in Guinea, consisting of shutters that pivoted and opened on the sea. In 1957 he started the Industrial Transport Equipment Company and built the Rotterdam Medical School, the Exhibition Center in Grenoble and the Orly Airways Terminal façade. In 1958 he collaborated on the design of La Maison du Sahara, a modern prototype of a house built for extreme climate conditions. Between 1952 and 1962 he collaborated with Jean Dimitrijevic on the Musée des Beaux Arts du Havre, a glass, steel and aluminum structure that received the Prix Reynolds in 1962.

21. There is a strong link between architecture and a better society. Architects are often very far-sighted intellectually,

they see their work as art and but this is art in a socially applied format. It is craving to see art with all its benefits taken from the confines of an art studio and an art gallery and placed in the world. In an applied situation the architect can then seek to raise the quality of their work and the concepts behind these to apply then to architecture and thus in some cases bring architecture to a very sensually appealing level.

22. *The German Ideology* p.111: "With them...it reflected not so much the actual fact but rather the desire to reduce all relations to the relation of exploitation, and to explain the intercourse of people from material needs and the ways of satisfying them. The problem was set. Hobbes and Locke had before their eyes both the earlier development of the Dutch bourgeoisie (both of them had lived for some time in Holland) and the first political actions by which the English bourgeoisie emerged from local and provincial limitations, as well as a comparatively highly developed stage of manufacture, overseas trade and colonization." And p.112 "At an earlier period of political economy had been the subject of inquiry either by financiers, bankers and merchants, i.e. in general by persons directly concerned with economic relations, or by person with an all-round education like Hobbes, Locke and Hume, for whom it was of importance as a branch of encyclopedic knowledge."

And from Engels on philosophy from letter to Conrad Schmidt October 27 1890. From *Marx and Engels Selected Correspondence* p.59:

"In philosophy, for instance, this can be most readily proved true for the bourgeois period. Hobbes was the first modern materialist (in the sense of the eighteenth century) but he was an absolutist at a time when absolute monarchy was in its heyday throughout Europe and began the battle against the people in England. Locke was in religion and in politics the child of the class compromise of 1688. The English deists and their more consistent followers, the French materialists, were the true philosophers of the bourgeoisie, the French were even the philosophers of the bourgeois revolution. The German philistinism runs through German philosophy from Kant to Hegel, sometimes in a positive and sometimes in a negative way. But the precondition of the philosophy of each epoch regarded as a distinct sphere in the division of labor, is a definite thought material which is handed down to it by its predecessors, and which is also its starting point."

23. Also in *Capital* Volume 1, as the division of labor, expressed philosophically, became part of the main economic structure, the specialization of the production process in manufacturing is charted by Marx, p.546:

"All work at a machine requires the worker to be taught from childhood upwards, in order that he may learn to adapt his own movements to the uniform and unceasing motion of an automaton."

Page 547; "Machinery is misused in order to transform the worker, from his very childhood, into a part of a specialized machine."

p548; "Factory work exhausts the nervous system to the uttermost; at the same time, it does away with the with the many-sided play of the muscles, and confiscates every atom of freedom, both in bodily and intellectual activity."

And p.614; "...large scale industry sweeps away by technical means the division of labor characteristic of manufacture, under which each man is bound hand and foot for life to a single specialized operation. At the same time, the capitalist form of large-scale industry reproduces this same division of labor in a still more monstrous shape; in the factory proper, by converting the worker into a living appendage of the machine; and everywhere outside the factory by the sporadic use of machinery and machine workers."

24. Rawlinson's grinding machine (Harley) is an example of an invention put into practice by Middleton the London colorman.

25. According to Cole (1983) there was no spiritual calling to becoming an artist in the guild system. Art was regarded as something that anyone could be taught, on a par with shoemaking. Artisan trades such as bookbinding, weaving, textile dyeing, glass blowing, shoemaking, drapery and printing were integrated with the fine arts skills of painting and sculpture. Many painters, for instance, were also members of the pharmacists guild.

26. "Despite capital investments the official art academies still faced increasing financial pressures from all sides throughout the nineteenth century. The student-teacher ratio more than doubled in most studios resulting in overcrowding and reduced personal tuition time."

27. Modeled upon the *French Academie de Peinture et de Sculpture*, which was founded by Louis XIV in 1648 and shaped by precepts laid down by Joshua Reynolds. In 1769, in the first year had 77 students. By 1830 there were 1,500 students, the intake of 25 students a year. Other students included John Landseer, William Blake, John Constable, JMW Turner, David Wilkie. As Barratt explains:

"Academies were originally organized by states to regulate the training and development of artists. In the broadest sense, they wrestled the production of art away from a guild controlled, church-sanctioned mechanism to an academic system sponsored by the state..." "This transition coincided with both a social and conceptual change in pedagogy, wherein art instruction shifted from the private to the public domain, and away from the practical and the theoretical."

28. Turner was the son of a hairdresser and brought up above his father's shop in London's Covent Garden. Then as now, a fashionable part of the city drawing thousands to the theaters and it was also the center for the colormans' trade where artists and theatricals bought their materials. Turner's precocious talent for drawing was nurtured by his father, who exhibited and sold young Turner's work from the shop. He showed a talent for drawing from an early age and as a boy earned money by coloring prints. In 1789 he began working as a draughtsman for the architect Thomas Hardwick, and later in the same year he enrolled at the *Royal Academy Schools*. He studied regularly until 1793 and intermittently until 1799. Early in his student days he also had lessons from Thomas Malton (1748-1804), a topographical watercolorist who specialized in neat and detailed town views and whom he later described as "my real master".

29. This mingles with Turner's own background in the world of fashion, as mentioned, his father's profession as a barber was a practical purveyor of style and a skilled craftsman also fully ensconced in the aesthetic industry. In Covent Garden in London the young Turner and his father would have been acquainted with the local colormen, tailors and costume makers, actors and other artistic professions that peppered the neighborhood. Today the descendents of this atmosphere still exist in the vicinity and it is still the place to go for art materials. Until a few years ago the best art materials supplier Cornellissen with multicolored jars of pigment lining its eighteen century shelves, was in Covent Garden, until it moved half a mile away to Bloomsbury.

30. This was to: "Take the bones of sheep's trotters, break them grossly and boil them in water until cleared from their grease, then put them into a crucible, calcine them and afterwards grind them to powder." (Hamilton 1997) This chalky powder was then combined with paint, and applied in a

mosaic of color patches over a rough sketch of the subject.

31. Turner evidently had a serious interest in science. He knew Babbage another local and also Faraday, Davy and Sommerville. Turner's membership of the Royal Society of Arts, formed to integrate artists and scientists with commerce, gave him contact with the world of science.

32. As this quote testifies: "He was interested in how different kinds of light obscured and presented subjects to him. A further change was the decision to start painting in oils, a medium he practiced with for four years before using on pictures for exhibition. Even though Turner did not follow any "school" of painting, his developing technique with oils shows the meticulous attention he paid to art's technical side." http://www.infobritain.co.uk/Joseph_Turner_Biogr aphy_And_Visits.htm

33. By the time Turner's abstract works were "accepted" by the art establishment the radical nature of abstraction was itself being molded into Cartesian assimilation by artists, writers and critics as part of the expressionist trace, the "very trace of the expressive body, and thus of the "human essence" ' to repeat Burgin. With the aid of such critics the more "dangerous" and non-Cartesian elements of Turner's works could now be overlooked. Yet twentieth century advancement regarding the nature of perception and the modernist aesthetic were initiated by the seminal aspect of Turner's method and approach. The radical potency of this remains today because the conditions of production still entail the separation of physical and mental labor and which also molds items of design produced under these conditions (Singh 2007). The work of Turner and other artists' also still function in radical opposition even now.

34. There are some notable examples of the narrative nature of Turner's work as political. *The Battle of Trafalgar* was Turner's one and only Royal Commission and the pictorial

narrative content of the painting caused a stir because of the 'morbidly' detailed dead body of the sailor placed in front of the glorious and noble battleship. This was judged to be in terribly bad form. It was against the grain to demonstrate death in such truthful detail in battle scenes and probably a major reason why Turner was excluded from all future commissions.

35. All of these scientists worked in areas that touch on perception and art. This includes Faraday and his analysis of the polarization of light and Davy's research into color in the essay *Some Experiments and Observations on the Colors used in Painting by the Ancients* which is still referred to by the National Gallery London's Technical Department today.

36. As Tedman says: "The function of the art ASA (Aesthetic State Apparatus) is simple in this understanding: it is to mediate the transactions, the 'traffic,' between Superstructure and Base. But by definition this mediation is not 'ideological' mediation, it is not the 'flow or exchange of ideas,' it is a different kind of traffic, it is sensual mediation, if you like: it is the technique of ideological mediation, or how ideology is transferred or transacted."

37. As Tedman also says: "The working classes, its representatives and fellow travelers feel differently about life than the bourgeoisie and already have a different position - way of acting that reveals this difference."

38. Benjamin specifies in *Art in the Age of Mechanical Reproduction* (2000 p.326) that: "It is significant that the existence of the work of art with reference to its aura is never entirely separated from its ritual function. In other words, the unique value of the 'authentic' work of art has its basis in ritual, the location of its original use value."

The technical aspect of Turner's work and its overriding affect and effect bears no relation to aura and ritualism and in fact diminishes a shamanistic relishing of the spirit, as

Benjamin might pronounce, in favor of a bodily response to his methods of construction and scientific investigation of perception. I suggest that Turner's contradiction to the aura is as potent as any photographer or film maker who themselves might succeed in implementing as ambitious a technical approach as Turner. Turner's work does not project a transcendental aura but an effectuality through material construction which is felt by the body. The continuation of the separation of artist from materials, the control of materials by large manufacturers and the implementation of the division of labor in general, even in this, our age of mechanical (and now digital) production, still make the ramifications of Turner's technique as pertinent as when he first painted.

Turner worked as a practitioner of visual art just as Benjamin worked as a practitioner of literary art as well as a theorist of literature, as a literary critic. His critical understanding and theorization of technique within literature is sourced from his own sensual and physical involvement in its creation. However as a critic who theorizes visual art, Benjamin is omitted from the position of practitioner and does not therefore have involvement with it on a technical level. So Benjamin is a rigorous materialist critic in the field of literary art, but with regard to visual art, he omits the implementation of his own stipulation of fully analyzing technique (such as is suggested in another of his essay's *The Author As Producer* 1983) and therefore of placing the art within the production relations of its time. The failure to seize the point of technique in painting, therefore regresses his thesis with regard to visual art until it is under the influence of the area Benjamin is able to criticize so precisely as the realms of his own subject: literature. With regard to visual art he is subject, to paraphrase Benjamin himself, (p.91): "to a radical understanding in terms of mentality without at the same time being able to think about its relationship to the means of production and its technique." Without this radicalism Benjamin labors under the traditional influences of writers such as Bellori and Winckelmann and subsequent writers. There again a reversion to the tradition of mainstream ideology of heralding the ritualistic, aura and transcendent genius misconstrued and reasserted with regard to all painting technique.

39.   As we mentioned earlier the result of this is that after Turner's death the wards of his estate found a number of unseen, non-figurative works at the studio and at this point did not realize they were paintings. After about 100 years these works began to be "valued". By then the radical nature of abstraction was itself being molded into Cartesian and transcendental emotional traces. Yet twentieth century advancement regarding the nature of perception and the modernist aesthetic were initiated by the seminal aspect of Turner's method and approach. Their radical potency remains today because the conditions of production still entail the separation of physical and mental labor of which Turner, among other artists', also function in radical opposition to.

40.   One difficulty rejecting this aspect of feelings in culture is that drugs, as aesthetic and physical requirements, are difficult to withdraw from. Cold turkey is always going to be nasty. For a generation brought up on populist cinema, popular music and television it is difficult to forget the moments of pleasure and release when the drug provided its temporary "hits". There is a resistance to distancing these feelings, and the memory of them *even* when they no longer becomes such an ardent necessity of the mode of production. Aesthetic transition goes much deeper into the formation of pain, pleasure and creativity, luxury and

distress after life long exposure. It is difficult to find an example to try to follow but perhaps the old Soviet Union yields some clues. As Tedman explains in his work on the Soviet avant-garde, the uneven development between the various levels means that art and its underdeveloped state has dragged the other levels such as economic, backward. This resulted in glasnost in the Soviet Union and the revival of pop/rock music, western style cinema, television and fashion. Perhaps it has something to do with the fact that, despite the many excellent conditions of production, many workers never got to the stage of a shorter working day for example. The opportunity never arose in this system to achieve less working hours and really break the division of labor at this level. This was a stage of socialism that never achieved more advanced levels of communism and hence perhaps the eventual resurgence, of western style popular music to alleviate the physical alienation of such production.

Bibliography

A

Anderson, Perry. 1998. *The Origins of Post Modernity*. London; Verso.

Althusser, Louis. 1969. *For Marx*, Reading Capital. Ideology and Ideological State Apparatuses. Verso.

For Marx. 1969. London; Verso.

1969. *Lenin and Philosophy*. 1969. Monthly Review Press.

Lisa Atkins and Beverley Skeggs. 2004. *Feminism after Bourdieu*. Blackwell Publishing.

Azzopardi, Paul and Cowey, Alan. December 1997. *Is Blindsight Like Normal, Near-threshold Vision?* Psychology. Volume 94. pp. 14190 - 14194

AVRC Clinical and Physiological Optics Research Group. City University website: www.city.ac.uk

B

Bailey, Anthony. 1997. *Standing in the Sun*. Harper.

Ball, Phillip. 2001. *Bright Earth*. London; Penguin.

Barrett, B. D. 2008. *North Sea Artist's Colonies*. Phd. Thesis. University of Groningen Digital Library.

Baudrillard, Jean. 1985. *The Ecstacy Of Communication*. In Postmodern Culture. Edited by H. Forster. London: Pluto Press.

Beachy, Robert and Roth, Ralf. 2007. *Who Ran the Cities (Historical Urban Structures) City Elites and Urban Power Structures in Europe and North America 1750-1940*. Ashgate.

Beasley, C. 1999. *What is feminism?: an introduction to feminist theory*. Unwin and Allen/books.google.co.uk.

Benhabib, Seyla. 1994 *Feminist Contributions: A Philosophical Exchange*. Routledge.

Bellori, Giovanni. 1995 *Lives of the Modern Painters, Sculptors and*

Artists. Phaidon.

Belting, H. (1984) 1995. *The End Of Art History?* In Art history and its methods: A critical anthology. Edited by. E. Fernie. London: Phaidon.

Benjamin, W., 2000. *Art in the Age of Mechanical Reproduction.* From The Continental Aesthetics Reader, Routledge: Taylor and Francis Group.2000, Edited by Clive Cazeaux

Benjamin, W., (1934) 1983. *The Author As Producer.* In Understanding Brecht. Translated by A. Bostock. London: Verso.

(1936) 2000. *Art in the age of Mechanical Reproduction.* In the Continental Aesthetics Reader, ed. C Cazeaux. London: Routledge.

1970. *One Way Street and other writings.* Verso.

Boyer, C. B. 1991. *A History of Mathematics.* Revised by Uta C. Merzbach. John Wiley and Sons, Inc.

Bentham, Jeremy. *Works of Jeremy Bentham.* Volume 2. Part2. Edited by Sir John Bowring, Google.books.fr

Bloch Ernst, (1959) 2000. *Artist Illumination As Visible Anticipatory Illumination.* In the Continental Aesthetics Reader, ed. C. Cazeaux. London: Routledge.

Bourdieu, Pierre. 1987. *Distinction: A social critique of the judgment of taste.* Translated by R. Nice. Cambridge, Mass.: Harvard University Press.

Bockemuhl, Michael. 1991. *Turner.* Taschen.

Brillat-Savarin, Jean Anthelme. 1838. *The Physiology of Taste.* Tessier.

Brodinak D. O. and Woods C. 2002. *Compelling Classroom Evidence That Link Visual System Anatomy.* Physiology and Behavior American Physiology Society.

Buchanan, R. A. 1992. *The Power of the Machine.* London; Viking.

Burckhardt, J. 1995. *Reflections on History.* Phaidon.

Burgin, V. 1992. *The End of Art Theory.* Macmillan.

Burke, Edmund. 1761. *A Philosophical Enquiry Into The Origins Of*

Our Ideals Of The Sublime And Beautiful. 3rd Edition. R and J Dodsley. www.google.book.fr

Burton, W. 1927. *Designing for Machine Made Goods.* London; Penguin.

Butler, J. 1990. *Gender Trouble.* Routledge.

1993 *Bodies That Matter.* Routledge.

C

Cennini, Cennino. 1954. *The Craftsman's Handbook.* Translated by D. V. Thompson, Jr. New York: Dover.

Chevalier, T. 1999. *Girl with a Pearl Earring.* London: Harper Collins.

Ian Chilvers, Harold Osborne, Dennis Farr. 1993. *The Oxford Dictionary of Art.* Oxford University Press.

Chomsky, Noam. 1964. *Current Issues in Linguistic Theory.* p.50 On the Notion "Rule of Grammar". From The Structure of Language: Readings in the Philosophy of Language, edited by Jerry A. Foder/Jerrold Katz, Prentice Hall, New Jersey, USA.

-1980. *Rules and Representations.* Basil Blackwell.

- 2000. *New Horizons in the Study of Language and Mind.* Cambridge University Press.

Clark, J. 1995. The Conditions of Artistic Creation. In Art history and its methods: a critical anthology. London: Phaidon Press.

Cole, Bruce. 1983. *The Renaissance Artist At Work.* John Murray.

Collet, Bernard. Youtube.com. *Interview.* Broadcast November 2011.

V J Cook. *Chomsky's Universal Grammar.* Blackwell. 1986?

Craske, M.1997. *Art in Europe 1700-1830.* Oxford University Press.

Csány V.. 2000. *The 'human behavior- complex' and the compulsion of communication: Key factors of human evolution.* Department of Ethology, University Budapest, Hungary. Semiotica 128-3/4. (p.45-60)

Cullen, Althea. 1993. *Techniques of the Impressionists.* London; Burlington Books.

Cumming, Elizabeth and Kaplan,Wendy. 1991. *The Arts and Crafts Movement.* London; Thames & Hudson.

D

Damasio, Antonio. 2006. *Descartes' Error.* Vintage Books.
- 2000. *The Feeling of What Happens.* A Harvest Book. Harcourt Inc.

D'Arcy Thompson. 1992. *On Growth and Form.* Canto Edition.

De Beauvoir, Simone. 2011 (1949).*The Second Sex.* Translated by Constance Borde and Sheila Malonvany. Knopf Doubleday.
- 1999. *She Came to Stay.* Norton W.W. and Company.

Delaware, Francois and Guineau, Elizabeth. 2000. *Color: The Story of Dyes and Pigments.* London; Thames and Hudson

Derrida, Jacques. 1985. *Freud and the Scene of Writing. Writing and Differance.* New York /London; Routledge Kegan Paul.
- 1985. *Cogito and the History of Madness.* Writing and Difference. Translated by G. C. Spivak. New York: Routledge and Keegan Paul.
-1994. *Specters of Marx.* Translated. P. Kamuf. New York: Routledge.
-1985. *Margins of Philosophy.* University of Chicago Press.

Descartes Rene.1989. *Discourse On Method.* Penguin Books.

Descartes, Rene.1992. *Discourse on Method.* J.M. Dent & Sons

Doerner, Max. (1921) 1970. *The Materials of the Artist.* Translated by E. Neuhaus. London: Granada.

E

Ebert, Teresa, 1995. *(Ultimately) Critique for Red Feminist. Post-Ality,* Marxism and Post-modernism. Maisonneuve Press.

Engels, Frederick.
-1941. *The Part Played by Labor in the Transition of Ape to Man.* From The Dialectics of Nature. Translated and Edited by Clemens Dutt. London; Lawrence and Wishart.
-1975. *Socialism: Utopian and Scientific.* Foreign Languages

Press. Peking.

-1977. *The German Ideology.* Lawrence & Wishart.

-1891. *Origins of the Family Private Property and the State.* English Translation made from the fourth German Edition. Foreign Languages Press. Peking.

-1868. *From letter written in April 1868.* Translated by Andy Blunden. Marx and Engels Complete Works. Volume 43. London: Lawrence and Wishart (p.541)

F

Febvre, Lucien. 1973. *A New Kind of History.* Edited by Peter Burke. London; Routledge Kegan Paul.

Finberg, A.J. 1961. *The Life of J.M.W. Turner R.A.* Oxford University Press.

Forty, Adrian. 1989. *Objects of Desire.* London; Thames and Hudson.

Freud, Sigmund.

-1979. *On Psychopathology.* Penguin.

-1985. (1920). *Beyond the Pleasure Principle.* On Metapsychology the Theory of Psychoanalysis. Penguin.

-1985. (1915). *Instincts and their Vicissitudes.* On Metapsychology the Theory of Psychoanalysis, Penguin Books.

-1985. (1915). *Mourning and Melancholia.* Penguin Books.

-1955. (1914). *An Infantile Neurosis.* From An Infantile Neurosis and other works. Vintage.

-1955. (1919).*The Uncanny.* From An Infantile Neurosis and other works. Vintage.

-(1919). *A Child is Being Beaten: A Contribution to the Origins of Sexual Perversions. Vintage.*

-1985.(1923) *The Ego and The Id.* From On Metapsychology the Theory of Psychoanalysis, Penguin Books.

-1984. *The Special Characteristics of the System Ucs.* Penguin Books.

G

Gage, J. 1987. *JMW Turner A Wonderful Range of Mind.* Yale University Press.

-1968. *Turner's Academic Friendships: C. L. Eastlake.* The Burlington.

Garfield, Simon. 2000. *Mauve: How One Man Invented a Color That Changed The World.* London; Faber and Faber.

Greer, Germaine. 1970.*The Female Eunuch.* MacGibbon and Kee.

-1999. The New Woman. Transworld.

Gombrich, Ernst. 1984. *The Story of Art.* London: Phaidon.

Guillaume, C G, Le Chanu, P and Zeder, O. 2001. *The little book of Vermeer.* Translated by S. Doris and C Weiner. Paris: Flammarion.

H

Hadjinicolaou, N. 1978. *Art history and Class Struggle.* Translated by L Asmal. London: Pluto.

Hamilton, J. 1998. *Turner and the Scientists.* Tate Gallery Publications.

- 1997. *Turner - A Life.* Sceptre.

Hardy, W. 1988. *The History and Techniques of the Great Masters: Turner.* Secaucus Chartwell.

Rosamund D. Harley. 1970. *Artists' Pigments 1600-1835.* London; Butterworths.

Hering, Ewald. 1964. *Outlines of A Theory of the Light Sense.* Translated by L M Hurvich and D Jameson. Cambridge: Harvard University Press.

Herrmann, L. Vol.9, No.2. *Exhibition Review.* Turner Studies p.51.

Rosemary Hennessy and Chrys Ingraham. 1997. *Materialist Feminism.* Routledge.

Hilbert, David R.. 1987. *Color and Color Perception.* Stanford CA.

Hill, David. 2008. Turner and Leeds. *Images of Industry.* Jeremy Mills.

Joanne Hollows and Rachel Moseley. 2006. *Feminism, Femininity and Popular Culture.* Manchester University Press.

Holmes, C. J. 1943. *Notes on the Science of Picture-Making.* London: Chatto and Windus.

Honderich, T. 1995. *The Oxford Companion to Philosophy.* Oxford University Press.

Hume, David. 1763. *An Enquiry Concerning Human Understanding.* From Essays and Treatise on Several Subjects. Printed for A Millar, A Kincaid, J Bell and A Donaldson. Edinburgh.

J

Jameson, F. 1985. *Postmodern Culture.* From Postmodern Culture. Edited by H. Foster. London: Pluto.

Charles Edward Jeanneret (Le Corbusier) and Amedée Ozenfant. 1990. *Purism.* From Art In Theory. Blackwell. Translation taken from Modern Artists On Art 1964.

K

Kant, Immanuel. 1787. *Critique of Pure Reason.* Translated by JMD Meilklejohn, Project Guttenberg.

Kirby, J. 1997. *Correspondence with Author.* National Gallery (London) Scientific Department.

Klein, Yves. 1974. *Selected Writings.* Edited by J & J. London; Tate Gallery Publications.

-*Long Live the Immaterial.* 2000 Edited by G. Perlien/B.Cora. New York; Delano Greenidge Editions. p.81, 82.

Kleiner, Fred S. and Maniya J. Kristin. 2005. *Gardner's art through the ages: the Western Perspective.* Wadsworth.

Kollontai, Alexander. 1921. *The Labor of Women in the Evolution of the Economy.* Selected Writings. Translated by Alix Holt. www.marxists.org

(1920). Communism and the Family. Selected Writings, Allison and Busby. Translated by Alix Holt, www.marxists.org

Kramarae C. and Treichler P. A.. 1996. *A Feminist Dictionary.* Pandora Press.

L

Lambert. 1986. *Color and Fibre*. New York; Shiffer Publications.

Lenin V.I. 1976. *Karl Marx*. Foreign Language Press.

Lewin, S. G. 1991. *Formica and Design*. Rizzoli.

Locke, John. 1721. *An Essay Concerning Human Understanding*. London. Printed for A Churchill at the Black Swan in Paternaster-Row and A Manship at the Ship

M

Mao, Tse-Tung. 1980. *Collected Works*. Peking Press.

Marchant, Joanna. Nov 14 1992. *Review: Insight Into Sight and Experience*. New Scientist, p.14

Marx, Karl

-1976. *Capital*. London: Penguin.

-1977. *Eighteenth Brumaire of Louis Bonaparte*. Norman Bethune Institute

-1987. *The German Ideology*. Lawrence & Wishart.

-1975. *Wages, Price and Profit*. Foreign Languages Press. Peking

-1978. *The Poverty of Philosophy*. Foreign Languages Press. Peking.

-1976. *Critique of the Gotha Programme*. Foreign Languages Press. Peking.

-1981. *Economic and Philosophical Manuscripts of 1844*. Translated by Progress Publishers. London: Lawrence and Wishart

-1976. *Thesis on Feuerbach*. From Ludwig Feuerbach and the End of Classical German Philosophy by Frederick Engels. Foreign Languages Press: Peking.

- 1973. *Preface to the Contribution to the Critique of Political Economy*. From Marx and Engels on Literature and Art. Marx and Engels Selected Works. Volume 1. Moscow p.p. 503-504.

Mayer, R. 1982. *The Artist's Handbook of Materials and Techniques*. London: Faber and Faber.

Millet, Kate.1969. *Sexual Politics*. Granada Publishing. Morris, William. 1934. Art and Socialism. London; Kelmscott Press. p.129

Mossman, S.. 1997. *Early Plastics Perspectives 1850-1950*. Leicester; Leicester University Press

Mueller, C G and R Mae. 1969. *Light and Vision*. Netherlands: Time-Life International.

N

National Gallery. 2001. *Press release for Vermeer and the Delft School Exhibition*.

Nietzsche, F. 2000. *On truth and lie in the extra-moral sense*. In Philosophy and truth: Selections from Nietzsche's notebooks of the early 1870s. Translated by D. Breazeale. In the Continental Aesthetics Reader, ed. C Cazeaux. London: Routledge.

Nochlin, Linda. 1989. *Women, Art and Power and Other Essays*. Thames and Hudson.

Norihoro, Sadato, Alvaro Pascual-Leone et al. 11 April 1996. *Activation of the primary visual cortex by Braille reading in blind subjects*. Nature Vol. 308 pp.526-528

P

Parker, Rozsika. Pollock, Griselda. 1981. *Old Mistresses. Women, Art and Ideology*. Pandora.

Who's Afraid of Feminism. 1997. Edited by Ann Oakley & Juliet Mitchell. Hamish Hamilton, London.

Pennington, D H. 1989. *Europe in the seventeenth Century*. London: Longman.

Helen Phillips, 7.2.2004. *Do we perceive using 'mindsight'?* New Scientist p.14.

9.9.2002. Vision enhances perception of touch New Scientist

Piaget, Jean. 1973. *Structuralism*. Routledge & Kegan Paul.

- 1979.*The Origin of Intelligence in the Child*. New York/London;

Routledge Kegan Paul.

Proust, Marcel. (1913) 2000. *Remembrance of Things Past.* Translated by T Kilmartin. In the Penguin Book of art writing, Edited by K. Wright and M. Gayford. London: Penguin.

Prouvé, Jean. 2001. *Par Lui-Meme.* Editions Du Linteau.

Q

Quine, Willard.Van Ormond. 1964. *Geometrical Objects.* from Problems of Space and Time. Editor J.J Smart, MacMillan.

R

Rensink, Ronald. January 2004. *Visual Sensing Without Seeing.* Psychological Science. Volume 15 p.27. Re: New Scientist, Feb 7 2004.

Reynolds, G. 1976. *Turner.* Thames & Hudson. p65

Robertson, Elliot. 1996. *Faith. Gender, Family and Society.* MacMillan Press.

Rose, Jacqueline. 1986. *Sexuality in the Field of Vision.* Verso.

Rowlands, A. 2001. *The Conditions of Life for the Masses.* Essay from Early Modern Europe: Edit. Cameron. Euan. Oxford University Press. The History of Design. London; Pluto Press.

Ashok Roy. 1997. *Correspondence with Author.* National Gallery London, Scientific Department.

Rutsky, R. L. 1999. *High Techne: Art and Technology from the Machine Aesthetic.* Minnesota University Press.

S

Sarnat and Nevsky. 1981. *Evolution of the Nervous System.* Oxford University Press. Ferdinand de Saussure. 1974. *General Course in Linguistics.* Fontana/Collins.

Schopenhauer, Arthur. 1986. *Essays and Aphorisms.* Penguin Classics.

Serres, Michel. 1982. *Turner Translates Carnot.* Block 6: Middlesex University Press.

Siegfried, A. 1930. *America Comes of Age.* London; Jonathon Cape.

Singh, I. Vermeer. 2004. *Materialism and the Transcendental in Art.* Rethinking Marxism.16/2.

- 2007. *Color, Facture, Art and Design.* Capitalism, Nature, Socialism. Volume 18.

- 1986. *Syntax and Semiology.* Degree Thesis, Portsmouth Polytechnic.

- Grounds and Paint, E-book, Published by Kindle

Spender, Dale. 1980. *Man Made Language.* Routledge Kegan Paul: Melbourne.

Spinoza, B. 1991. *The Ethics of Spinoza.* Edited by D. D. Runes. New York: Citadel Press.

Spooner, Shearjashub. 1867. *A Biographical History of the Fine arts: Being Memoirs of the Lives.* New York: Laypoldt and Holt. Digitized by University of Michigan.

Stafford, Cliff. 1998. *The English Archive of Design and Decoration.* Harry N. Abrams.

Steele, Jeffery. *Against Logocentricism,* Lectures and studio based tutorials Portsmouth Polytechnic 1983-1986

Stocker, Alan and Simoncelli. August 24 2009. *Visual Motion after-effects arise from a cascade of isomorphic adaptation mechanisms.* Journal of Vision.

T

Tedman, Gary. 2012. *Aesthetics and Alienation.* Zero Books.

-1999. *The Aesthetic Level of Practice.* Rethinking Marxism. 11/4.

-2004. *Subjectless Aesthetic.* Rethinking Marxism. 16/1.

-2004. *Karl Marx's 1844 Manuscripts as a Work of Art.* Rethinking Marxism 16/3.

-28.1.2009. *The Concept of "Aura" and the Question of Art in Althusser, Benjamin and Greenberg.* Political Affairs

-2010. *The Origins of Kitsch.* Rethinking Marxism 21/1

-1996. *Walter Benjamin and the possibilities of a productive aesthetic.* Detours and Delays. University of Derby

Thornbury, Walter. 1962. *The Life of J.M.W Turner*. Hurst and Blacket.

Dawson Stephens, Michael. 1988. *Culture, Education and the State*. Routledge.

Townsend, Joyce H. 1999. *Turner's Painting Techniques*. Tate Gallery Publishers.

Turner's Painting Methods a Preliminary Discussion. Turner Studies, Vol.10 No.1 (pp23-33)

V

Valenti, Jessica. 2007. *Full Frontal Feminist*. A Young Woman's Guide to Why feminism Matters. Seal Press, Routledge.

W

Walker, John A.. 1989. *Design History and the History of Design*. Pluto Press.

Wehlte, K. 1975. *The Materials and Techniques of Painting*. London: Vos Nostrand Rienhold.

Wells, H. G. 1927. *The Time Machine*. Collected works, Ernest Benn.

-1993. *The First Men on the Moon*. Everyman Library.

- 2005. *The Island of Doctor* Moreau. Penguin.

Werry, Chris. 2007. *Chomsky, Linguistic Discourse and the Value of Rhetorical self-consciousness*. Language Sciences.

William David. 2010. *UK Cities: A Look At Life and Major Cities in England, Scotland and Wales*. New Africa Press.

Wilson, Richard Guy and Pilgrim, Dianne H.. 1986. *The Machine Age In America*. Brooklyn Museum; New York.

Winckelmann, J.J. 1995. *The History of Ancient Art*. Phaidon.

Wittig, Monique. 2005. *Monique Wittiq: theoretical, political and literary essays*. Edited by Namascar Shaktini. Urbana: University of Illinois Press.

Woodham, Jonathon M. 1997. *Twentieth-Century Design*. Oxford; Oxford University Press.

Wolfflin, Heinrich. 1950. *Principles of Art History.* Dover Publications Inc. Translated by Hottinger.

Woolf, Naomi. 1990. *The Beauty Myth.* Vintage.

Contemporary culture has eliminated both the concept of the public and the figure of the intellectual. Former public spaces – both physical and cultural – are now either derelict or colonized by advertising. A cretinous anti-intellectualism presides, cheerled by expensively educated hacks in the pay of multinational corporations who reassure their bored readers that there is no need to rouse themselves from their interpassive stupor. The informal censorship internalized and propagated by the cultural workers of late capitalism generates a banal conformity that the propaganda chiefs of Stalinism could only ever have dreamt of imposing. Zer0 Books knows that another kind of discourse – intellectual without being academic, popular without being populist – is not only possible: it is already flourishing, in the regions beyond the striplit malls of so-called mass media and the neurotically bureaucratic halls of the academy. Zer0 is committed to the idea of publishing as a making public of the intellectual. It is convinced that in the unthinking, blandly consensual culture in which we live, critical and engaged theoretical reflection is more important than ever before.